Getting the Best Out of

SUPERVISION

IN COUNSELLING AND PSYCHOTHERAPY

SAGE has been part of the global academic community since 1965, supporting high quality research and learning that transforms society and our understanding of individuals, groups and cultures. SAGE is the independent, innovative, natural home for authors, editors and societies who share our commitment and passion for the social sciences.

Find out more at: **www.sagepublications.com**

⑤SAGE

Getting the Best Out of

SUPERVISION

IN COUNSELLING AND PSYCHOTHERAPY

A GUIDE FOR THE SUPERVISEE

🦋 🦋 🦋

MARY CREANER

⑤SAGE

Los Angeles | London | New Delhi
Singapore | Washington DC

SAGE

Los Angeles | London | New Delhi
Singapore | Washington DC

SAGE Publications Ltd
1 Oliver's Yard
55 City Road
London EC1Y 1SP

SAGE Publications Inc.
2455 Teller Road
Thousand Oaks, California 91320

SAGE Publications India Pvt Ltd
B 1/I 1 Mohan Cooperative Industrial Area
Mathura Road
New Delhi 110 044

SAGE Publications Asia-Pacific Pte Ltd
3 Church Street
#10-04 Samsung Hub
Singapore 049483

Editor: Kate Wharton
Editorial assistant: Laura Walmsley
Production editor: Rachel Burrows
Copyeditor: Sue Ashton
Proofreader: Jill Birch
Indexer: Avril Ehrlich
Marketing manager: Tamara Navaratnam
Cover design: Lisa Harper
Typeset by: C&M Digitals (P) Ltd, Chennai, India

© Mary Creaner 2014

First published 2014

Library of Congress Control Number: 2013940540

British Library Cataloguing in Publication data

A catalogue record for this book is available from the British Library

ISBN 978-0-85702-905-8
ISBN 978-0-85702-906-5 (pbk)

To Stephen
Tá mo chroí istigh ionat
Mo chuid den tsaol

Contents

List of Figures and Tables

About the Author

Mary Creaner is an Assistant Professor and Research Coordinator with the Doctorate in Counselling Psychology and Course Director for the MSc/Postgraduate Diploma in Clinical Supervision at Trinity College Dublin. She began her career in education, and subsequently qualified as a psychotherapist and clinical supervisor. Mary has been involved in developing and delivering a variety of postgraduate, professional development training and adult education programmes in this area for over 25 years. Mary is an accredited therapist and supervisor with the Irish Association for Counselling and Psychotherapy (IACP) and a member of the American Psychological Association (APA) Division 17 (Counselling Psychology) and APA Supervision and Training Special Section. Mary has a particular interest in clinical supervision theory, practice and research, which was the subject of her doctoral enquiry. She has written a number of publications and has presented her work nationally and internationally.

Acknowledgements

I believe that all writing endeavours are, by their nature, collaborative enquiries. Consequently, there are a number of acknowledgements that I wish to make. First, many thanks to the supervisees and supervisors with whom I have worked for the learning they have facilitated. They continue to inspire my work and my reflections on supervision. Thanks also go to past and present students of the Doctorate in Counselling Psychology and the MSc/Postgraduate Diploma in Clinical Supervision, Trinity College Dublin.

Many thanks go to my colleagues, Dr Ladislav Timulak, Barbara Hannigan and colleagues. Sincere thanks to Dr Rita Honan for the many supervision-related consultations over the years. Many thanks to Dr Anne Davis for the ongoing reflections. A special word of thanks to Eileen Boyle for her continual sharing of her infinite wisdom, for support and for continuing reflective conversations. Also to Marcella Finnerty for her constant encouragement and many offers of help.

Special thanks are also owed for the many learning conversations over the years regarding supervision research and practice, particularly to Prof. Maja O'Brien, Prof. Robert Bor, Dr Alison Strasser and Dr John Sharry.

Heartfelt thanks in appreciation of family, particularly my mother, Nuala, and of friends, who have been constant in their encouragement to begin and end this project!

Thanks also to Alice Oven, who initiated this book, and to Kate Wharton for her vast patience, encouragement and support throughout the process. Many thanks to Laura Walmsley and Rachel Burrows of the editorial and production teams at Sage Publications.

About the Book

Getting the best out of supervision requires both the supervisor and supervisee to invest much time, preparation, reflection, negotiation and active participation. It is a collaborative endeavour. It also means that supervisees are entitled to expect and will, it is hoped, receive the best supervision possible. To that end, this book provides a variety of considerations regarding the supervision experience, whether for the supervisee who is about to embark on a supervision relationship for the first time in their training experience, a continuing trainee or a post-qualification and experienced practitioner. It seeks to review the current landscape of supervision in terms of the benefits, opportunities and challenges that are evident. As supervisors, in the context of counselling and therapy (both terms are used interchangeably throughout the text), are frequently career-long supervisees, the information and reflections provided in each chapter may serve to stimulate critical reflection on how they may also optimally use supervision. It is also relevant for supervisors, particularly beginning supervisors, with respect to facilitating effective supervision from the supervisee's frame of reference.

The aim of this book is to provide information on the key supervision concepts and also to provide opportunities to reflect on these as they pertain to each supervisee's unique supervision situation. The book is not intended as a supervision manual; rather, it has been informed by the current literature and developed from many conversations with supervisees and supervisors regarding the principles of best practice. The themes that are presented have arisen from these conversations, and the book seeks to provide an integrative perspective on the art and science of supervision from my experience as a practitioner-researcher of dwelling in the in-betweens of science and practice. This text draws on current research and professional literature in the area of supervision and on my experience both as a supervisor and as a supervisee.

Considering the multitude of approaches to supervision, individual supervisor styles, theoretical orientations and preferences, together with work contexts, the welfare needs of the client, the learning needs of the supervisee, the variation in supervisor training among supervisors, current evidence in supervision and therapy, it is no wonder that the landscape of supervision, particularly for beginning supervisees, may seem like dragon territory. The following chapters seek to provide a research-informed map of the current landscape of supervision, with the systemic caveat that the map is never the territory! Each supervisory arrangement is a unique, negotiated encounter between supervisor and supervisee within the context of the work.

Chapter 1: What is the Meaning and Purpose of Supervision?

This chapter provides an orientation to the landscape of supervision by providing an overview of its historical development within the counselling and psychotherapy tradition. It will also discuss the purpose and functions of supervision as articulated in a number of existing definitions.

Chapter 2: The Supervisory Relationship: A Relationship with a Purpose

The supervisory relationship is identified as the central component in supervision and will be discussed with reference to Bordin's (1983) working alliance model. This chapter also outlines some of the phenomena and some of the challenges that may be encountered in the supervisory relationship and reviews how these may be conceptualised.

Chapter 3: Supervision across the Career Lifespan

This chapter considers the supervisee experience from a professional and research perspective, and highlights some of the key issues in supervision across the career lifespan. It includes both trainee and experienced practitioner perspectives.

Chapter 4: The Learning Landscape: Lifelong Learning in Supervision

This chapter reviews some of the key adult learning concepts as they pertain to learning in supervision. It also considers the means by which learning is best facilitated and the professional knowledge required for supervision practice.

Chapter 5: Models and Frameworks of Supervision

This chapter provides an introduction to some of the current supervision models and frameworks, as an example of how a supervisor might view a supervision session, and highlights areas of supervisory enquiry. An example of how a supervision framework may be used by the supervisee to prepare for and reflect upon their supervision session is discussed.

Chapter 6: Forms and Formats of Supervision

This chapter presents an overview of group, peer and live supervision, and considers the use of technology in supervision with reference to online supervision.

Chapter 7: Beginning the Learning Relationship

This chapter will develop the perspective of the supervisory relationship as a learning relationship within both a training and post-training context. It considers the professional boundaries that are necessary to establish and maintain a supervision relationship. It provides guidelines for developing a learning agreement with a supervisor with reference to individual supervisee contexts.

Chapter 8: How to Prepare for a Supervision Session

This chapter has a practical, 'how to' focus, and refers to the process knowledge required of a supervisee. Some strategies are suggested to prepare for and maximise learning in supervision.

Chapter 9: Ethical and Legal Considerations in Supervision

This chapter provides an overview of some of the key ethical considerations in supervision, including informed consent, confidentiality, multiple relationships, disclosure and record keeping as they pertain to the supervisee–supervisor relationship. Equality and inclusive practice is reviewed as it relates to supervision, and the well-being of the supervisee is considered.

Chapter 10: Good and Not So Good Supervision

This chapter will explore effective and ineffective supervision with reference to the key purposes of supervision: primarily, the well-being of the client and the professional development of the supervisee. With these in mind, the chapter will consider some of the impacts and outcomes that supervision has for clients and supervisees. It also considers how supervisee and supervisor contribute to effective or ineffective supervision as reported in the literature.

Chapter 11: Professional Considerations in Supervision

This chapter will focus on issues related to professional practice, including fitness to practise and professional standards in supervision. It provides an example of the accreditation requirements for supervision from the perspective of the British Association for Counselling and Psychotherapy (BACP). It presents some of the current debates regarding the benefits and challenges of professionalisation in the field.

Chapter 12: Feedback and Evaluation in Supervision

Giving and receiving feedback are discussed from the perspective of the supervisee and supervisor and as a strategy to facilitate learning. The evaluation task in supervision is also presented, and key issues regarding this task are considered.

Chapter 13: Endings in the Learning Relationship and the Opportunities Ahead

This chapter will reflect on a much-neglected area in the literature: namely the ending of a supervisory relationship and contract. It will also outline continuing professional development with reference to supervision training. Supervision competencies and key areas for consideration in supervision training curricula are also discussed.

Chapter 14: Developing the Art and Science of Supervision

This chapter considers some of the current issues regarding the art and science of supervision and proposes some areas for further research and development. It also provides reflection on the practitioner as researcher and what that means in the context of supervision.

Appendices

The appendices aim to provide useful resources for supervisees and supervisors:

1   Sample supervision learning agreement
2   Session pro forma documents
3   Codes of ethics and best practice guidelines for supervision
4   Supervision conferences
5   Sample of supervision training courses
6   Key journals for supervision-related articles
7   Sample of international organisations
8   Supervision resources on the Internet
9   Holloway's (1995) process matrix
10   Helpful Aspects of Supervision forms
11   Sample of professional associations: accreditation/registration organisations

Introduction

This book originated in my seeking to understand the complex phenomenon of supervision, initially as a supervisee and subsequently as a supervisor, trainer of supervisors and researcher practitioner. From my experience and research, I have come to understand supervision in the context of psychological therapy as a complex activity and intricate relationship, the process of which is dynamic, paradoxical and synergetic. All of my experiences have undoubtedly influenced and shaped how I think and feel about supervision and how I apply it in practice. However, what was most influential and formative for me were those initial experiences as a supervisee.

By way of background, and in an attempt to declare my own biases and assumptions regarding supervision, I should explain that my career began in education in the early 1980s and this was my first encounter with supervision as a trainee educator. Informed by the dominant psychological theories and philosophical discourses of the day, it was a particularly exciting time in the development of learning theory (or perhaps it seems so in retrospect as it was *new* learning to me). This, in turn, informed pedagogy and andragogy, the methods of teaching and learning of the time. The ideas of Carl Rogers and student-centred learning had entered the lexicon of education and were formative in my development as an educator. Informed also by social and political contexts, it was a time when education for social justice became part of the general discourse through the work of Paulo Freire, and feminist theories began to shine light on issues of equality and power. As this informed my professional development at that time, so too was it brought forward and further developed when I was a first-time supervisee during my therapy training in the early 1990s.

My initial experiences of supervision in a therapy context were very positive, and I found it a most helpful and validating experience. I still do. Supervision was a place where I could bring my doubts and concerns, where the sharing of these was welcomed, where mistakes were seen as part of the learning journey, and where the client was held firmly at the centre of this learning. I think I was fortunate at that time to have worked with supervisors who had dedicated training in supervision and who were aware of supervision as a professional activity that was distinct from therapy. The working relationship was characterised by respect and collaboration and was well balanced between support and challenge. Learning in supervision was an enjoyable experience. Ultimately, the supervisors with whom I worked were a good match in terms of style, focus, process and authenticity.

In retrospect, like many trainees I have since encountered, I recall being concerned that my neophyte trainee position and lack of experience would impact negatively upon the client. I experienced supervision as providing a safety net for both the client and myself. I was also mindful that I was being evaluated on my work, but as this was explicitly contracted within my training course and negotiated with the supervisor, it became an integral part of the work. As an educationalist, I understood that the evaluation of learning outcomes is a given in the learning process. Furthermore, it was conducted collaboratively, based on my learning needs and congruent with my developmental stage. Any concerns I had regarding power differentials were mediated by the quality of the relationship. It was not that issues did not arise; rather, that there was sufficient psychological safety to work through them. Overall, I felt well supported and appropriately challenged in the work. In retrospect, perhaps it all sounds an ideal; however, while I do expect that there is some 'narrative smoothing' (Spence, 1986: 211) at play, my abiding sense remains that I had a positive experience of supervision and I assumed that this was the norm.

Post-training, my experience of supervision has been for the most part a very useful and productive endeavour but not, naturally, without some anomalies. I have worked with a few supervisors who had limited understanding of what supervision was or, indeed, what it could be. In those instances, I recall frustration and some indignation as it was a costly enterprise. However, the enduring feeling was one of missed opportunities for deeper learning. In one or two of my experiences with supervisors, there was nothing, in essence, that I could name as an issue, but the pairing just did not work for me or perhaps for us both.

In terms of my professional development as a supervisor, my motivation to train arose from the belief that, while learning from experience was necessary, it was not sufficient in itself. In my own practice, I had found supervision worthwhile and useful. It provided and continues to provide me with a reflective space for my professional development and personal well-being. As a practitioner, it is one of the few places where I, as professional self, can bring all the parts of my work and reflect on these holistically.

So I come to supervision from a background of education and psychotherapy, and conceptualise supervision as a meeting place for both. However, supervision is not therapy, nor is it education, but the knowledge base and processes involved in each have relevance for supervision from my perspective. Each speaks to the uniqueness of the individual, to facilitative and collaborative learning relationships, to growth and development. This meeting place is also reflected in my professional context. I have been involved in the training of counsellors and therapists for over 20 years, and have been engaged in providing training to supervisors for over ten years.

The aim of supervision in the context of my educational experience was to facilitate me to apply theory to practice artfully by creating conducive learning relationships and environments, consider individual or group learning needs, implement methods of teaching and learning with reference to the learning context, and evaluate those methods in terms of process and outcome. It was a firm foundation on which to build. Psychotherapy training, and subsequent supervision and research training, enhanced and expanded that view to reflect in depth on the person of the supervisee and supervisor, the quality of the relationship and, most centrally, the needs of the client, which is the main purpose of supervision. Supervision always occurs within a context, and the context of the work also needs to inform supervision. Multiple contexts exist for the supervisor, supervisee and client, and, from a systems perspective, a feedback loop exists whereby each informs the other (for example, professional, research, ethical, economic, political, social).

There are many ways to supervise, and each supervisor and supervisee will have their own styles and approaches. My approach to supervision has been informed by all of my life experiences and learning to date. As a therapist, my theoretical orientation is integrative, informed by psychodynamic, cognitive-behavioural and systems approaches which are significantly underpinned by a humanistic perspective. My supervision approach clearly draws on this foundation, but I consider supervision as a professional activity distinct from therapy and, ideally, as a collaborative learning relationship.

As I bring myself to practice and, indeed, to research, my assumptions, beliefs and worldview influence how I conceptualise and practise supervision. In summary, and to frame the supervision approach that informs this text, the following ten assumptions are made:

1. Effective supervision is a useful professional activity (Wheeler and Richards, 2007).
2. Client welfare and positive therapy outcomes are the primary purpose of supervision (Ellis and Ladany, 1997).
3. The professional development and learning needs of the supervisee are central to supervision (Holloway, 1992; Watkins and Scaturo, 2013).
4. In supervision, the supervisor and supervisee are both learners as well as knowers (Phillips and Kanter, 1984; Creaner, 2008).
5. The supervision relationship is more than a relationship, it is a working alliance, with an emotional bond, goals and tasks to be agreed and effected (Bordin, 1983).
6. Supervision is collaborative learning in relationship (Creaner, 2011a).
7. Critical reflection is the medium of learning (Carroll, 2009).
8. The focus of supervision is on learning from reflective practice (Argyris and Schön, 1974) to improve practice and develop practice-based knowledge.
9. Supervision holds the potential for transformational learning (Carroll, 2010).
10. Supervision is about 'travelling curiously' (Lidmila, 1997: 44).

1

What is the Meaning and Purpose of Supervision?

This chapter provides an orientation to the landscape of supervision by providing an overview of its historical development within the counselling and psychotherapy tradition. It will also discuss the purpose and functions of supervision as articulated in a number of existing definitions.

What is Supervision?

Beginning trainees bring many questions to supervision, most notably: 'What is supervision?' 'Why is it necessary?' and 'What happens in supervision?' They are essential, reflective practice questions and, in many ways, remain a focus of enquiry throughout the career lifespan. As the supervision conversation continues to develop through practice and research, new ideas emerge and new ways of working are presented. As I have developed as a practitioner, the type of supervision I have sought has also developed from formative to consultative supervision as I focus on the broad context of my work. As suggested by Stoltenberg (2005: 858), 'the path toward proficiency is developmental.' Different learning needs emerge as supervisees gain knowledge and capability (Stoltenberg and McNeill, 1997). It may also be developmental for supervisors as they gain knowledge and clinical wisdom.

It is challenging to define supervision. It has different meanings in different contexts. For example, from a professional perspective, in counselling and therapy training it is an integral part of the training process and embedded in that context. It is supported by formal teaching and, frequently, personal therapy. In this context, it is most clearly evaluative, as trainee competence development is keenly monitored in client work. Post-training, as a counsellor or therapist works towards accreditation or registration, while there is more autonomy, supervision is still evaluative. Post-accreditation/registration, and as supervision is usually a career-long requirement, there is a shift towards more consultation and less evaluation. Nevertheless, the element of 'overseeing' is always present. However, to present supervision in these terms only does not do justice to the supervision phenomenon. It does not capture the essence of the interpersonal supervisory relationship. Nor does it speak to the experience of the learning process that is at the heart of supervision and how that occurs in relation to the vicissitudes of that experience. The following section demonstrates the complexity of the supervision endeavour and presents some of the attempts to capture the meaning and purpose of supervision.

In answer to the question 'What is supervision?' from a professional practice perspective, the British Association for Counselling and Psychotherapy (BACP, 2008) provides the following explanation:

> Supervision is a formal arrangement for therapists to discuss their work regularly with someone who is experienced in both therapy and supervision. The task is to work together to ensure and develop the efficacy of the therapist/client relationship. The agenda will be the therapy and feeling about that work, together with the supervisor's reactions, comments and challenges. Thus supervision is a process to maintain adequate standards of therapy and a method of consultancy to widen the horizons of an experienced practitioner.

The British Psychological Society (BPS) Division of Counselling Psychology, in their *Guidelines for Supervision* (BPS, 2007: 4), also provide a useful definition and frame to reflect on the complexities of supervision when they describe it as an 'activity', a 'process', a 'relationship' and a 'practice'. As described by the BPS, it is a professional and ethical activity for reflection on the work that allows for 'playful reflection' for the purposes of future action and is distinct from therapy. Supervision is a process of 'ongoing collaborative, experiential and transformational learning' that draws on practice and research-based knowledge. It is a 'flexible' relationship of 'mutual trust, respect and integrity' that takes into account the learning needs of the supervisee. Finally, it is a practice that is bounded by an explicit contract and draws on 'shared and explicit models of supervision' (BPS, 2007: 40).

The meaning of supervision and how it is implemented in counselling and psychotherapy have evolved significantly over many decades, but the key purpose has remained relatively constant. In essence, supervision exists to facilitate the professional development of the supervisee at whatever their level of experience with a view to enhancing therapy outcomes with their clients (Ellis and Ladany, 1997). To understand the meaning and purpose of supervision, it is necessary to consider how it has evolved historically in the field and to review the dominant definitions that have developed in an attempt to elucidate the meaning and purpose of supervision in counselling and psychotherapy.

Historical Overview of Supervision

The concept of supervision has existed almost as long as the therapy profession itself. The development of supervision within psychotherapy can be more or less charted against developments in psychotherapy theory and practice (Leddick and Bernard, 1980). With its roots in the apprenticeship model, wherein the master passed on their knowledge and skill to the apprentice, as soon as therapists began to provide training to other therapists, supervision frameworks began to emerge within therapy traditions (Leddick, 1994). The development of supervision is chronicled by Carroll (2007: 34), who highlights three stages in the development of supervision occurring broadly within three timeframes, namely: (1) the 1920s and the foundations of the psychoanalytic tradition; (2) the 1950s and the emergence of the humanistic/existential and cognitive-behavioural schools; and (3) the 1970s when supervision began to emerge as a learning activity rather than a counselling activity.

The foundation of the Berlin Institute in the 1920s heralded the emergence of supervision in this context (Leddick and Bernard, 1980; Bernard, 2006; Carroll, 2007). Freud has been acknowledged as the 'first supervisor' (Frawley-O'Dea and Sarnat, 2001: 17) within psychotherapy, a point contested by Milne (2009), who suggests that the apprenticeship model has been in existence for centuries and that the origins of supervision may perhaps be traced back to the ancient Greeks – at the very least! As psychoanalytic training developed, so too did the concept of supervision, or 'control analysis' as it was termed, which sought to maintain the purity of the approach (Moncayo, 2006). It was in the 1930s that the 'teach or treat' controversy arose, and it remains a point of discussion to this day. Bernard and Goodyear (2009: 82) identify Ekstein and Wallerstein (1958) as the first proponents of a psychodynamic supervision model that 'portrayed supervision as a teaching and learning process' which placed emphasis on the teaching rather than the analytic treatment of the supervisee.

Against a backdrop of social, cultural, economic and political events, the 1950s were a fertile time in the development of the psychotherapy profession and, consequently, saw the second stage of the development of supervision. The most notable development that culminated during this period was the emergence of the humanistic, existential and cognitive behavioural schools, most evidently captured in the iconic film *Three Approaches to Psychotherapy* (1965), more affectionately referred to as the 'Gloria' film, produced by E.L. Shostrom, which demonstrated the respective therapeutic approaches of Carl Rogers (person-centred therapy), Albert Ellis (rational emotive behavioural therapy) and Fritz Perls (Gestalt). Carroll (2007: 34) refers to supervision during this period as being 'counselling-bound or psychotherapy-bound' supervision wherein the principles of the therapeutic approach are applied to the practice of supervision. By the mid-1960s, according to Leddick and Bernard (1980: 190), 'the field of supervision had three major models: dynamic, facilitative, and behavioural.' Family therapy had also made the valuable contribution of a systems perspective to therapy and also to supervision. With its foundations firmly established in the therapy tradition, influenced by a variety of cross-theoretical concepts, supervision in therapy began to develop its own unique identity. The 1970s saw a further shift away from a counselling conceptualisation of supervision to one that focused more on supervision as 'an educational process' with social roles models that focused on practice (Carroll, 2007: 34). The development of supervision is continuing, theory is slowly developing and supervision is beginning, though not without its challenges, to establish its own knowledge base.

Definitions of Supervision in Counselling and Psychotherapy

A myriad of terms has been applied to supervision, and confusion is frequently compounded by misunderstandings regarding the nature of supervision. In the literature, we hear of counselling supervision, clinical supervision, training supervision, consultancy, professional supervision, peer, group and individual supervision and so forth. In addition, supervision may mean different things in different contexts, all of which may have a bearing on where emphasis is placed and how supervision is effected. In the vernacular, supervision is often negatively connoted with line management supervision – literally, 'overseeing' – with the managerial agenda of performance review for promotion purposes and career development. However, there are an increasing number of definitions available and the following are an example, though by no means exhaustive, of those currently in use. Some will be relevant to particular supervisee developmental levels more than others. Each definition has its own nuances, emphasis and applicability to a range of contexts in the helping professions, though few are empirically based (Milne, 2009).

Two of the most frequently provided definitions in counselling and psychotherapy are those of Inskipp and Proctor (2001) in the UK context and Bernard and Goodyear (2009) in the US. Inskipp and Proctor (2001: 1) proposed that supervision is:

> A working alliance between the supervisor and counsellor in which the counsellor can offer an account or recording of her work; reflect on it; receive feedback and where appropriate, guidance. The object of this alliance is to enable the counsellor to gain in ethical competence, confidence, compassion and creativity in order to give her best possible service to the client.

Clearly, the emphasis here is on the working alliance in counselling, a concept first proposed by Bordin (1979, 1983) which refers to collaborative goal and task setting in the context of an emotional bond between the relevant parties, in this case the supervisor and supervisee (see Chapter 2 for further discussion). Within the working alliance, which is a central tenet in this definition, the work is reflected upon and feedback is provided in the interest of the professional development of the supervisee and client welfare. While not explicit, the inclusion of 'guidance' intimates an educative dimension to supervision. The language of 'compassion' and 'creativity' attests to the art of supervision (Hewson, 2001).

Aligned to Inskipp and Proctor's (2001) definition are the three functions of supervision offered by Proctor (1987) which have been widely drawn upon as a framework in practice in counselling, therapy and nursing supervision (Bowles and Young, 1999). It is a particularly useful framework for considering the purpose of supervision. Drawing on Kadushin's (1992) framework (given in parenthesis), Proctor's (1987) three functions relate to the following domains:

1. *Formative* (*Educative*) relates to supervisee learning, skills development and professional identity development.
2. *Normative* (*Managerial*) refers to accountability, developing best practice principles, ethical and legal considerations, compliance with agency and organisational procedures and professional standards for the well-being of clients.

3. *Restorative* (*Supportive*) considers the impact of the work on the supervisee and the necessary psychological support and scaffolding required to offer professional support to the supervisee. This function can help mitigate the stresses and impacts of the work and promote practitioner well-being.

With reference to the US context, where supervision has predominantly been conceptualised in a counselling education and training context, Bernard and Goodyear (2009: 7) posit that:

> Supervision is an intervention that is provided by a more senior member of a profession to a more junior member or members of that same profession. This relationship is evaluative, extends over time, and has the simultaneous purposes of enhancing the professional functioning of the junior person(s), monitoring the quality of professional services offered to the clients she, he, or they see, and serving as a gatekeeper for those who are to enter the particular profession.

Within this definition, a threefold perspective is provided wherein professional development, client welfare and gatekeeping are emphasised in the context of training. This definition highlights the hierarchical nature of the supervisory relationship which develops over time, monitors and evaluates the supervisee in their provision of therapy. The context of training is also reflected in the assumption that the supervisor is a more senior member within the same profession. The task of teaching is implicit with the 'idiosyncratic nature' of the supervisees' learning needs as the guiding agenda (Bernard and Goodyear, 2009: 9).

Relevant to post-training supervision, Scaife (2001) emphasises a formally contracted supervisory arrangement to reflect on one's practice for the purpose of client welfare and the professional development of the supervisee. Scaife (2001: 4) offers the definition that supervision is 'what happens when people who work in the helping professions make a formal arrangement to think with another or others about their work with a view to providing the best possible service to clients, and enhancing their own personal and professional development'. A more specific definition from a competency-based perspective is provided by Falender and Shafranske (2004: 3), who acknowledge that supervision is a distinct intervention and activity when they state:

> Supervision is a distinct professional activity in which education and training aimed at developing science-informed practice are facilitated through a collaborative interpersonal process. It involves observation, evaluation, feedback, the facilitation of supervisee self-assessment, and the acquisition of knowledge, and skills by instruction, modelling and mutual problem solving. In addition, by building on the recognition of the strengths and talents of the supervisee, supervision encourages self-efficacy. Supervision ensures that clinical consultation is conducted in a competent manner in which ethical standards, legal prescriptions, and professional practices are used to promote and protect the welfare of the client, the profession and society at large.

This comprehensive definition emphasises a strengths-based and collaborative view of the supervisory relationship which is focused on education and training for the purposes, again, of professional development and client protection. It uniquely refers to science-based practice development, and highlights some of the key tasks and strategies employed in supervision. It further evokes a systems perspective.

Emphasising the educative dimension of supervision, Bradley and colleagues (2010: 3) define supervision as follows:

> Counselor supervision is a didactic and interpersonal activity whereby the supervisor facilitates the provision of feedback to one or more supervisees. This feedback can pertain to the work in supervision, the supervisees' clients, or the supervisor, and can positively or negatively influence supervisee counselor competence and client outcome.

Interestingly, this is one of the few definitions that suggest that supervision may negatively influence supervisee development or outcomes for clients.

With an emphasis placed on the educational aspects of supervision and reflective practice, Hart (1982: 12) offers the following definition of supervision as 'an ongoing educational process in which one person in the role of the supervisor helps another person in the role of the supervisee acquire appropriate professional behavior through an examination of the supervisee's professional activities'. More recently, Watkins (2012: 193), echoing Hart's (1982) emphasis on the educational process, proposes that supervision is 'an educative process by which and through which we as supervisors strive to *embrace, empower, and emancipate* the therapeutic potential of the supervisees with whom we have the privilege to work' (emphasis in original). Evocative of Freire's (1970) concepts of empowerment and emancipation achieved through education, theory and praxis are interesting concepts in supervision, particularly in relation to power and advocacy for social justice.

While many definitions of supervision exist, very few have been empirically validated. An exception to this is the definition offered by Milne (2009), who draws on the definitions of Inskipp and Proctor (2001) and Bernard and Goodyear (2009) presented above. Milne (2009: 439) proposes that supervision is:

> The formal provision, by approved supervisors, of a relation-based education and training that is work focused and manages, supports, develops, and evaluates the work of a colleague/s. It therefore differs from related activities, such as mentoring and therapy, by incorporating an evaluative component and by being obligatory. The main methods that supervisors use are corrective feedback on the supervisees' performance, teaching and collaborative goal-setting. The objectives of supervision are 'normative' (e.g. case management and quality control issues); 'restorative' (encouraging emotional experiencing and processing); and 'formative' (maintaining and facilitating the supervisee's competence, capability and general functioning).

The reference to 'approved supervisors' suggests that some agreed standard of proficiency is required of the supervisor. This definition also makes an explicit statement on the educative dimension of supervision wherein the provision of feedback is seen as the means of facilitating supervisee development with reference to the normative, restorative and formative functions of supervision. Evaluation is provided through corrective feedback on performance and competence.

Supervision can serve normative, restorative and formative functions. With reference to the training context and the 'pre-registration' stage, Scaife (2001: 4) considers additional features of supervision which facilitate professional identity development for the supervisee, communication of the norms and standards of the profession and the gatekeeping role of the supervisor. Scaife also acknowledges the power differentials present in the supervisory relationship and the potential impact of evaluation on the supervisee. However, within counselling and therapy, the latter features are ever present in the career lifespan (although perhaps to a lesser extent post-accreditation) when supervision is mandated as a requirement for accreditation by a professional body and external monitoring in that regard is a continuing requirement for practice.

In the context of counselling and therapy, supervision provides for four core functions, according to Grant and Schofield (2007: 3):

1. The acquisition and improvement of therapeutic skills and knowledge.
2. Quality control and accountability to the client and to the public.
3. Transmission of the culture of psychotherapy, including ethical behaviour.
4. Professional development and growth.

Common Factors

As you can see, many definitions of supervision exist in the field and, as mentioned, all seek to capture the essence and critical components of the complex supervisory relationship and process. While there is no consensus on a particular definition, all speak in some way of supervisee development and client welfare. Scaife (2001: 4–5) summarises these key components well when she suggests that the 'features of supervision' are specific to the purpose of supervision which is to secure the welfare of clients and enhance best practice and service to clients. To this end, the focus of supervision is primarily on the needs, experiences and professional development of the supervisee. Furthermore, supervision occurs in the context of a formal, contracted relationship characterised by mutual trust and respect (see Chapter 7). This relationship excludes other role relationships or, when this is unavoidable, these are explicitly negotiated. Many of the definitions presented provide some insight into what can happen in supervision. In presenting their client work, the supervisee will receive feedback and be given guidance to help them develop competence in their role as a counsellor or therapist.

In summary, supervision serves a number of related functions. It primarily exists for the welfare of the client, the professional development of the supervisee and gatekeeping for those who enter and continue to work in the profession. By providing gatekeeping, through the monitoring of the professional development of the supervisee with the overall goal of continuing competence development in the role of the counsellor or therapist (Holloway, 1992), supervision seeks to offer protection to the client and to the public. It also seeks to provide for the welfare of the supervisee by giving support in professional identity formation and affording some containment for the stresses of the work. Interestingly, few definitions refer to the potential development of the supervisor as a consequence of their provision of, and mutual engagement in, the supervisory relationship and process (Carrington, 2004). In addition, few make any explicit statement about the need for this professional relationship to be informed by research. Furthermore, whether implicitly or explicitly stated, the supervision relationship or working alliance is at the heart of supervision. Within that working alliance, there are tasks to be accomplished and goals to be achieved, as will be discussed in Chapter 2.

Supervision among the Helping Professions

It is important to note that the therapy context and setting in which supervision occurs (for example, a training institution, statutory or voluntary agency, private practice) may require further consideration. For example, as noted by the BACP (2008: 2), 'agencies and institutions may have their own criteria for supervision and provide supervisors from within the organisation.'

Supervision is not the prerogative of counselling and psychotherapy, although the long tradition of its existence can mean that it is often taken for granted 'as a given' within our profession. Other disciplines, particularly those in the applied areas, have also embraced supervision as a means of facilitating professional development and client welfare. For example, social work has a long tradition of supervisory practice (Davys and Beddoe, 2010). Many disciplines within mental health (for example, nursing) are continuing to develop supervision models relevant to their contexts. From an interprofessional perspective, therapists/supervisees working in multidisciplinary teams may be challenged by the lack of a shared meaning of supervision which has yet to be established. However, what seems to be generally agreed is that supervision exists for client welfare and the professional development of the supervisee (Cutcliffe et al., 2001; Munson, 2002).

REFLECTIVE QUESTIONS

1. Of the definitions provided, which appeals to you most and why?
2. What do you see as the main purpose of supervision? To you as a supervisee? To your clients? To the counselling and therapy profession?
3. What do you see as the key elements of supervision?
4. How does your supervisor define supervision?
5. How do you define supervision?
6. If you were to identify a metaphor or image of good supervision, what would that be?

2

The Supervisory Relationship: A Relationship with a Purpose

The supervisory relationship is identified as the central component in supervision and will be discussed with reference to Bordin's (1983) working alliance model. This chapter also outlines some of the phenomena and some of the challenges that may be encountered in the supervisory relationship and reviews how these may be conceptualised.

The Supervisory Relationship

Most definitions of supervision acknowledge the central importance of the supervisory relationship and it appears to be a common factor among all. The quality of this professional relationship is paramount to good supervision; it is the context in which supervision takes place (Holloway 1995). The supervision literature is replete with testimony to the centrality of the relationship (Worthen and McNeill, 1996; Watkins, 1997; Stoltenberg et al., 1998; Nelson and Friedlander, 2001; Weaks, 2002; Beinart, 2012), which has been confirmed more recently in the study of Ladany and colleagues (2013: 14), wherein the supervisory relationship is identified as a 'critical component' in effective supervision. In a study conducted with trainees, Worthen and McNeill (1996: 29) contend that the quality of the supervisory relationship was the 'pivotal and crucial component of good supervision experiences'. They identified a good supervisory relationship as one that invited openness to learning, and was characterised by empathy, non-judgement, validation, affirmation and an attitude that permitted exploration and experiment.

Akin to therapy, the establishment of a good relationship in supervision contributes to good outcomes (Horrocks and Smaby, 2006; Bucky et al., 2010; Norcross, 2011). An effective supervisory relationship is positively associated with supervisee self-efficacy (Efstation et al., 1990) and supervisee self-disclosure (Ladany et al., 1999; Adair, 2001;

Hess et al., 2008). It is a dynamic process that occurs in a triadic relationship of supervisor, supervisee/therapist and client. It is further informed by the relationships that surround the context of supervision. With reference to the task of evaluation, Worthen and Dougher (2000) report that the supervisory relationship is significant in creating an environment conducive to effective evaluation. This is further supported by Lehrman-Waterman and Ladany (2001) who inferred that evaluation conducted within a supportive relationship may have the effect of strengthening the therapeutic relationship.

In an attempt to capture a complex interpersonal process, different descriptions of the supervisory relationship are provided throughout the literature. Holloway (1995: 41) discusses the supervisory relationship as the 'core factor' and a 'container of dynamic process' for supervision. The relationship encompasses all the elements of supervision (for example, tasks and functions). In her systems model of supervision, Holloway (1995) proposed that the relationship comprises interpersonal structure, phases (beginning, maturing and ending) and contract (see Chapter 7). The structure refers to the interpersonal and relational aspects of how the supervisor and supervisee will work together over the course of a supervision contract which seeks to explicate roles, rights and responsibilities within the relationship (see Figure 5.1 on p. 43 for Holloway's systems model).

As will be noted frequently throughout this book, the process of supervision is a complex professional activity, and the supervisory relationship is no less complex. Many variables exist within the relationship, all of which need to be taken into account (supervisee factors, supervisor factors, client factors) and further mediated by the myriad of contexts (theoretical, developmental, cultural, ethical, legal and so forth) of practice.

When speaking with some trainee therapists recently, and enquiring about their general experience of the supervisory relationship, each described their experience quite differently. Many referred to the personal qualities of the supervisor (she was very approachable; he understood and listened to me; she did not seem all that interested in my work). Others mentioned their supervisor's expertise (he is very experienced with the client group I am working with; she is not very familiar with my theoretical orientation), while others spoke of the impact of the experience on them as supervisees ('I'm really learning a lot'; 'It is a great support for me and my clients'; 'I feel judged a lot of the time'). Many factors and variables influence the quality of the supervisory relationship, most particularly supervisor factors, supervisee factors, client factors and organisational contexts.

The Learning Relationship and Working Alliance

The supervisory relationship is a relationship with a purpose; it is a learning relationship to enhance therapist effectiveness for positive therapy outcomes. Applying his therapeutic working alliance model to supervision, Bordin (1983) discussed the supervision working alliance as characterised by the development of an emotional bond (attachment) between the supervisee and supervisor, agreed supervision goals and supervision tasks. While it is a facilitative relationship, it is also a relationship with a purpose. In his working alliance model of supervision, Bordin (1983: 37–8) proposed that the goals of supervision to be facilitated with the supervisee relate to the following:

1. The mastery of specific skills.
2. Enlarging one's understanding of the client.
3. Enlarging one's awareness of process issues.
4. Increasing one's awareness of self and impact on process.
5. Overcoming personal and intellectual obstacles towards learning and mastery.
6. Deepening one's understanding of concepts and theory.
7. Providing a stimulus to research.
8. Maintaining standards of service.

These clearly relate to the goals of therapist training and continuing professional development. It is interesting to note that Bordin (1983: 38) makes explicit reference to the goal of supervision as a 'stimulus to research'. In the current discourse of evidence-based practice and practice-based evidence, it is apposite that a research attitude is fostered and promoted in supervision and therapy.

With reference to the tasks of supervision, Bordin (1983: 38) recommends that the supervisee needs to undertake a number of tasks to prepare for and actively participate in supervision. The preparation of a verbal or written case report of the client work to be reviewed and direct observation of the supervisee's work through recordings are recommended. Bordin (1983) assigns responsibility for selecting specific issues or difficulties for review to the supervisee. The role of the supervisor within this model is that of a 'coach', helping the supervisee to focus on key areas, identifying gaps, offering alternative perspectives on the issues brought, and providing feedback, all with a view to increasing the supervisee's developmental direction.

Factors that Influence the Working Alliance in Supervision

As supervision occurs in a relationship, the behaviours of both the supervisor and the supervisee contribute to the working alliance. Bernard and Goodyear (2009: 159) have identified six such supervisor behaviours, namely:

- the supervisor's style;
- how they use power (see Chapter 10);
- their use of self-disclosure;
- the nature of their attachment style;
- how they conduct evaluation (see Chapter 12); and
- how they behave ethically (see Chapter 9).

In acknowledgement of the fact that it is the supervisor rather than the supervisee who holds primary responsibility for the working alliance, Bernard and Goodyear (2009: 160) note that more attention has been given in the literature to supervisor factors in this regard, but that two supervisee variables, 'secure attachment' and 'supervisee negative experiences' (Chapter 10), have been found to contribute to the working alliance. Of the supervisor behaviour identified by Bernard and Goodyear (2009), the following sections will consider the supervisor's style, the attachment style of both supervisor and supervisee, and supervisor self-disclosure. How supervisors use power, how they conduct evaluation, how they behave ethically, and the negative experiences of supervisees are discussed in subsequent chapters as indicated (in parentheses) above.

Supervisor Style

The style of the supervisor relates to what (content) the supervisor focuses on in supervision and how (process) they do so in the supervisory relationship. It refers to the supervisor's unique way of interacting with the supervisee and of effecting supervision (Friedlander and Ward, 1984; Ladany et al., 2001) and also the role the supervisor adopts in their approach to supervision.

The interpersonal and relational nature of the supervisory relationship has been characterised by many of the qualities of the therapist–client relationship. Relational contact, trust, empathy, non-judgement, congruence and genuineness are the familiar person-centred conditions of a facilitative relationship (Rogers, 1951) and the creation of a facilitative learning environment. The profile of the ideal supervisor as presented in the literature is a multidimensional picture relating to personal qualities, behaviours and attitudes. The positive personal qualities identified are analogous to those of the ideal therapist characterised by warmth, empathy, congruence and a non-judgemental attitude (Rogers, 1951; Carifio and Hess, 1987). In addition, Bucky et al. (2010: 149) identified a number of supervisor positive qualities that contributed to the perceived quality of supervision from the perspective of the supervisee, namely, having 'above-average intelligence, a positive attitude toward themselves, ethical integrity, and strong listening skills'. Other qualities apparent refer to the supervisor's enthusiasm, positive energy, sense of humour and competence (Carter et al., 2009); their flexibility and ability to empower and validate the supervisee (Gazzola and Theriault, 2007); their capacity to normalise the supervisee's experiences (Worthen and McNeill, 1996; Haugaard Jacobsen and Tanggaard, 2009;); and whether they provide constructive feedback (Gazzola and Theriault, 2007), allow for mistakes to be made (Hutt et al., 1983) and are committed to supervision (Wulf and Nelson, 2001). Areas for improvement were identified by Bucky and colleagues (2010: 159) as 'awareness of countertransference in supervision, the ability to stay focused, the ability to meet time constraints, commitment to the supervisory alliance, and an ability to challenge the supervisee effectively'.

In developing a Supervisory Styles Inventory (SSI), Friedlander and Ward (1984: 541) identified three supervisor styles as 'attractive', 'interpersonally sensitive' and 'task oriented'. The 'attractive' domain includes qualities such as supervisor friendliness, warmth, flexibility and supportiveness. An 'interpersonally sensitive' style would demonstrate, for example, supervisor perceptiveness, creativity, intuition and resourcefulness in working with a supervisee. On the other hand, a 'task-oriented' style would include an approach practically focused on goals in a structured, didactic and evaluative manner. These styles correspond with Bernard's (1979) three supervisor roles of *consultant* (e.g., resourcing the supervisee to facilitate their learning and develop autonomy); *counsellor* (e.g., supporting supervisee development); and *teacher* (e.g., didactic approach), respectively (Bernard, 1997: 312). Not surprisingly, the attractive and interpersonally sensitive styles contribute to stronger working alliances (Bernard and Goodyear, 2009). Crook Lyon and Potkar (2010: 26) suggest that supervisors 'need to have the flexibility to engage in a variety of supervisory styles and roles' across various levels of supervisee experience to optimise the supervision working alliance and enhance supervisee self-disclosure of material relevant to supervision (Mehr et al., 2010).

Supervisor Self-disclosure

'Self-disclosure' can be defined as the sharing of personal information about oneself. At one level, we are constantly disclosing information about ourselves in the way we present and dress and in our non-verbal communication and so forth. Related to the concept of professional boundaries, and with reference to therapy, there has been much controversy about the therapist's intentional self-disclosure to clients, frequently mediated by the practitioner's theoretical orientation (Ziv-Beiman, 2013). Other factors that influence self-disclosure in therapy relate to therapist factors, client factors and cultural variables (Farber, 2003). Therapist self-disclosure has frequently been seen as a potential 'slippery slope' continuum from boundary crossing to ultimate boundary violation (Glass, 2003). Consequently, supervisors may be inclined to hold the same boundary, to the same extent, in supervision, particularly with trainees. Other perspectives refer to the potential usefulness of appropriate and judicious self-disclosure which is immediate and relevant to the client and may have the effect of enhancing the therapeutic relationship (Ziv-Beiman, 2013).

Similarly, in supervision, the degree to which supervisors appropriately self-disclose has been perceived to impact positively on the supervisory working alliance (Ladany and Lehrman-Waterman, 1999). Supervisor self-disclosure may also provide modelling to supervisees and encourage their self-disclosure of information pertinent to their therapy work or the supervisory relationship (Adair, 2001; Knox et al., 2008, 2011).

Mindful that supervision is also a professional relationship, Ladany and Walker (2003: 612) refer to five categories of personal disclosure which provide a framework for supervisors in this regard:

- personal material;
- therapy experiences;
- professional experiences;
- reactions to the trainee's (supervisee's) clients; and
- supervision experiences.

Each category is mediated by the relevance of the disclosure to the learning needs of the supervisee, whether it is an 'intimate' or 'non-intimate' disclosure, and whether or not it is congruent for the supervisor (Ladany and Walker, 2003: 612). The supervisor's appropriate sharing of information related to their own experiences of training, challenges in the work, reactions to the supervisee's clients, their own professional journey, and how they experience the supervisory relationship may help normalise the supervisee's experience. Ladany and Walker (2003) caution, however, that over-disclosure, particularly of personal material, may have a negative impact on the supervisee, and suggest that it is useful to consider whether the disclosure directly contributes to supervisee learning.

Supervisee and Supervisor Attachment in Supervision

Among the many psychoanalytic concepts that have become part of the general vocabulary of supervision, the concept of attachment is quite prevalent in the literature. Drawing on the attachment theory work of Bowlby (1969) and Ainsworth (1969), it is suggested that attachment patterns may be a useful consideration for supervision (Watkins 1995; Neswald-McCalip, 2001; Pistole and Fitch, 2008; Dickson et al., 2011) and is another way to consider the emotional bond to which Bordin (1983) refers. Three attachment styles have been observed in infants and were identified as *secure*, *avoidant* and *ambivalent* (Ainsworth, 1969). In essence, and in very simple terms, attachment behaviour seeks secure attachment to a primary caregiver which, if reasonably successful, results in a sense of well-being and safety for the child. In turn, the caregiver develops a reciprocal bond and provides a secure base from which the child can explore the world in the knowledge that it is safe to do so and that there is a secure base to which the child can return (Bowlby, 1988; Pistole and Fitch, 2008). Conversely, if the caregiving is persistently unavailable or unreliable, the child, in response to the stress evoked, will anxiously retreat or withdraw. The self is organised in relation to the other, and attachment systems are internalised; hence, they become the child's working model of the world and the lens through which they perceive subsequent relationships (Lamagna, 2011). Attachment systems may also be considered as a template for adult relationships (Renfro-Michel and Sheperis, 2009).

From this perspective, anxiety will activate attachment behaviours. In addition, Bowlby (1969) proffered the idea that particular problematic attachment patterns were evident among individuals who experienced persistent parental rejection or over-control. When the caregiver is experienced as indifferent or emotionally unavailable, specific behaviours may be employed to mitigate further rejection (for example, compulsive self-reliance, compulsive caregiving and anxious attachment patterns of compulsive care-seeking and angry withdrawal).

Focusing on these behaviours as they pertain to supervision, Watkins (1995), in acknowledging that supervision may be an anxiety-provoking experience for trainees which activates attachment behaviours, provides a description of supervisee compulsive self-reliance behaviours which include 'a supervisee who

- may even refuse or resist help either directly or indirectly,
- believes he or she knows best, has the answers well in hand,
- is resentful of supervision and the supervisor,

- unrelentingly questions or challenges the supervisor's comments or suggestions,
- proceeds as he or she wants in therapy and informs the supervisor after the fact, and
- though being defiant, resentful, disparaging, and derogatory, still desperately wants the supervisor's approval of what he or she has done (as a therapist trainee) and is deeply wounded when any disapproval or alternate suggestions are forthcoming' (Watkins 1995: 335).

Similarly, Watkins (1995) contends that a supervisee who displays compulsive caregiving and anxious attachment patterns may become overly dependent on the supervisor, constantly seeking help, presenting with regular crises or becoming angry with the supervisor. In all situations, such attachment-seeking behaviours can negatively impact on the supervisory relationship and consequently upon the therapeutic relationship. Watkins (1995) further suggests that personal therapy is a more appropriate forum for these issues to be addressed, as the context of supervision may in itself exacerbate these behaviours, which may ultimately indicate that the supervisee is not yet ready to engage in the supervisory process and perhaps in the therapeutic process with clients.

Supervisees who display secure attachment behaviours in supervision contribute positively to the supervisory working alliance by establishing relationships with their supervisors that are characterised by openness and trust and are appropriately help-seeking when dealing with challenges in their client work (Renfro-Michel and Sheperis, 2009). The attachment styles of supervisees as a predictor of professional development were investigated in a study by Foster and colleagues (2007), who conducted their enquiry with supervisor/supervisee dyads ($n = 90$). Their findings revealed that supervisees' patterns of attachment to their supervisors were similar to attachment patterns in their other relationships. Interestingly, they discovered that supervisees who displayed insecure attachment to their supervisor also self-reported poorer professional development. However, the supervisor rated their professional development levels more positively. The authors suggest that supervisee self-assessment may be influenced by the perceived accessibility and support of the supervisor.

There is little information available on the attachment patterns of experienced practitioners. However, in the training context, no differences were found across trainee developmental levels (i.e., beginning trainees were no less secure than more experienced trainees), but supervisees with more secure attachment orientations reported a stronger bond with their supervisors (Renfro-Michel and Sheperis, 2009).

What has been conspicuous by its absence in the literature is comparable treatment of the supervisor's attachment style. Pistole and Fitch (2008: 196) observe that 'for a supervisee, the supervisor may be the preferred caregiver when stresses or anxieties are related to counselling sessions and training experiences.' Consequently, the implication is that the supervisor needs to respond to the supervisee's anxiety, provide containment and a secure base so that the supervisee can proceed to explore and learn. This is to assume that supervisor attachment behaviour is secure. The potential exists for problematic attachment patterns to be negatively reinforced if they evoke counter-transferential feelings in the supervisor or if the supervisor has insecure or ambivalent attachment patterns. Gilbert and Evans (2000: 92) propose that the supervisor needs to be 'well-grounded' in their 'secure attachment patterns' to facilitate a positive learning process for the supervisee.

Supervision may provide a reparative and restorative relationship for supervisees and can help buffer the stresses of the work (Proctor, 1987; Gilbert and Evans, 2000). Furthermore, as Fitch and colleagues (2010) outline, supervisee insecure attachment behaviours can provide opportunities for a supervisor to provide grounding and establish a secure base for their learning. Even when particularly difficult situations arise for a supervisee – for example, as offered by Fitch et al. (2010: 30), when a trainee attachment style interferes with their learning to the extent that they have not developed the requisite competency to practise and the 'gatekeeping responsibilities' of the supervisor need to be evoked – effective supervision may provide a secure base in which they may explore a remedial development plan or, in some instances, an alternative career plan.

It is important to note that not all feelings of insecurity are problematic, and even practitioners with the most secure attachment behaviours may feel insecure at times, irrespective of their professional experience. It is a normative response to feel apprehensive about meeting a client for the first time or to feel anxious about a client who is at risk or when grappling with an ethical dilemma. It is natural at times to contend with one's feelings of incompetence or to feel overwhelmed in response to witnessing human suffering. It would be more problematic if this work did not evoke our human responses.

Psychological Safety in Relationship

Psychological safety is frequently referred to as a necessary condition in the supervisory relationship (Emerson, 1996; Weaks, 2002; Carter et al., 2009). The psychoanalytic concepts of 'holding' (Winnicott, 1960) and 'containing' (Bion, 1962; Casement, 1985) have also become familiar terms in the professional language of supervision. The 'cyclical model' of supervision (Page and Wosket, 2001) is described by the authors as 'a container for creativity and chaos' (Wosket and Page, 2001: 19). These concepts evoke images of parent and child in a safe environment. 'Mother' can provide for 'child' when another adult is supporting her (Hawkins and Shohet, 2012); the implication being that the supervisee needs to be supported in their role as therapist and counsellor and that supervision can provide a secure base for their learning. Holding evokes intimate proximity-seeking and, as Gilbert and Evans (2000) advise, humility and awareness on the part of the supervisor are required to manage the power base implied in this relationship. In that proximity-seeking, the tasks and goals of supervision mediate professional boundaries.

Parallel Process

Linked to the psychoanalytic concepts of transference and counter-transference, 'parallel process' is another familiar concept in supervision literature and appears to be generally accepted across theoretical orientations. With reference to the *transference* process in therapy, this phenomenon relates to an unresolved issue or an element of the relationship dynamics with a significant other from early life being unconsciously projected or transferred onto the therapist in the present. From the classical psychoanalytic perspective, the more blank the therapist screen, the more likely that transference will develop and become the phenomena to be worked through and resolved in the analytic relationship. By the same token, *counter-transference* is when the client's transferential feelings may activate reactions and feelings in the therapist which may relate to their own personal history. Hence, therapist self-awareness is key to mitigate the acting out of counter-transferential reactions. From this perspective, such awareness can also provide useful insights into the client's phenomenological world.

Parallel process was first described by Searles (1955: 135) as a process of reflection, whereby 'processes at work currently in the relationship between patient and therapist are often reflected in the relationship between therapist and supervisor' and consequently regarded as information for supervisee learning. Later, Ekstein and Wallerstein (1972) saw the supervisory relationship as a mirror of the therapeutic relationship, with the supervisee unconsciously bringing dynamics of their therapy relationship into supervision. In other words, parallel process refers to the 'unconscious replication of the therapeutic relationship in the supervisory situation' (Morrissey and Tribe 2001: 103). Many theorists, both within and outside the psychoanalytic tradition, acknowledge the occurrence of parallel process (for example, Doehrman, 1976; McNeill and Worthen 1989; Jarmon 1990; Raichelson et al., 1997) and supporting evidence has been identified by Tracey and colleagues (2012). Nevertheless, it remains a controversial concept with many cautions apparent in the literature and many variations on the conceptualisation and causes of this phenomenon. On the one hand, parallel process has been referred to as an illusion (Lesser, 1983); on the other hand, 'parallel process often offers a didactic opportunity and a powerful tool for the supervisor to use regardless of theoretical orientation' (Haugaard Jacobsen, 2007: 32).

Parallel process can also be seen as bi-directional: just as therapist/client dynamics may be re-enacted in the supervisory relationship, so the dynamics of the supervisor/supervisee relationship may also be played out in the therapist/client relationship (Doehrman, 1976; Tracey et al., 2012), a worrying thought if the supervision relationship is problematic. Whichever direction the parallel process is going, the therapist/supervisee is seen as the conduit of transfer. Furthermore, the similarity between the structure of supervision and that of therapy lends itself to hierarchical positions, with the supervisee presenting as help-seeking and the supervisor seen as help-giving, and issues of authority frequently implicated in considerations of parallel process (Mothersole, 1999; Morrissey and Tribe, 2001). Lombardo and colleagues (1998) emphasise that supervisors need to know how to work with parallel process in supervision and how to use it to facilitate supervisee learning. Carroll (1996: 103) advises that parallel process ought not to be seen as a 'magical formula for clever interpretation' by the omnipotent supervisor, but may best be used to facilitate learning for the supervisee through, for example, role-play. Similarly, from a relational theorist's perspective, over-focusing on parallel process in supervision may obscure complex client dynamics and undermine the supervisory relationship (Miehls, 2010).

Seeking psychological safety may also be thought of as a parallel process in supervision. Just as the client seeks psychological safety from the therapist, so too may the supervisee seek safety from the supervisor. The theme of safety brings to the foreground what is potentially unsafe in supervision for supervisee, supervisor and client, and the profound responsibility that is inherent in the role of the supervisor. It illuminates the shadow aspect from two angles. If supervision is experienced as 'too safe', risk avoidance may impede the learning and professional development of the supervisee and the therapeutic experience of the client. On the other hand, if a lack of safety is experienced by the supervisee, it too may impede learning and negatively impact upon supervision and consequently on therapy.

Ruptures and Repairs in the Supervisory Relationship

All human relationships hold the potential for conflict or, in Bion's (1979: 247) terms, 'an emotional storm'. Given the 'evaluative, yet clinical nature of the relationship', conflicts arising in supervision are not uncommon (Nelson et al., 2008: 172). However, it is the management of that conflict that either contributes to individual or interpersonal growth and development or, conversely, negatively impacts upon the supervisee or supervisor. The management of that conflict, as advised by Nellis and colleagues (2011: 7), is the responsibility of the supervisor and 'the productive management of conflict can improve the supervisory experience and strengthen the relationship.' This presumes that both parties are open to addressing conflict where it arises. Good supervision, according to Crick (1991: 236), 'does not consist solely of what is provided by the supervisor; it is also the result of an interaction between a particular student and supervisor; and some pairings just do not work.'

Conflict seems to be widely evident when things go wrong in supervisory relationships and when, as McCarthy Veach (2001: 396) states, 'relationships are less than ideal'. There are many reasons why conflict can arise in the real relationship of supervision, ranging from personality characteristics, relational dynamics and transferential/countertransferential reactions to the other, through attachment styles and differences in goal or task agreement to role ambiguity. It may also arise due to differences of opinion between supervisor and supervisee regarding case conceptualisation and differing theoretical approaches to client work.

A psychodynamic perspective would explore conflict as an enactment of conflict in the therapeutic relationship, or as parallel process as it manifests in the supervision session. However, while conflict may be a parallel process, it is important not to assume that it is, as doing so may result in disengagement from the responsibility of addressing the issue and consequently disengagement from the relational aspects of the supervisory relationship (Safran et al., 2007).

Inevitably, all supervisees will potentially encounter ruptures in the supervisory relationship over the course of their career, just as they will encounter ruptures in the therapeutic relationship in their work with clients. While it is considered the supervisor's responsibility to manage conflict, the literature purports that, in some instances, supervisors lack the competency required in this regard or may not be aware of emerging issues if undisclosed by the supervisee (Nelson et al., 2008). Interestingly, less experienced supervisors may experience more conflict in the supervisory relationship (Quarto, 2003).

It is reported that, while supervisees initially perceive conflict in supervision to have a negative impact on the supervisory relationship, open discussion of these issues can have the effect of enhancing the relationship (Nelson and Friedlander, 2001; Quarto, 2003). Likewise, Carroll and Gilbert (2011: 136) propose that dealing with conflict can be an opportunity for learning, and offer a number of strategies for supervisees to deal with conflict in supervision. Among them, they propose that a supervisee can reflect on the conflict and also on their contribution to the issue. Clarity regarding the supervision contract is also regarded as a method of clarifying roles, rights and responsibilities in supervision. Carroll and Gilbert (2011) encourage the supervisee first to attempt to address the conflict with the supervisor. In the event of that not being possible, it could be discussed with a colleague, peer or, if in a training context, with a tutor or the course director. Should it be a matter of unethical or harmful supervision, then a complaint to the supervisor's accrediting or professional body may be warranted. However, as this may have serious consequences, it is important that the matter be given due process and ethical consideration with due regard to potential legal implications (for example, libel, slander). Consultation that provides support for the supervisee's decision-making is recommended. The supervisor should be made aware that a complaint has been made, and discussion of how best to address this would be a matter of professional consultation.

Conflict does not always equal a negative event, and it would also be problematic if differences in worldview did not sometimes meet in this dynamic working relationship. When relationship rupture is managed productively and repaired within a secure base in supervision, it can provide modelling for the repairing of inevitable ruptures in therapeutic relationships (Safran et al., 2007).

REFLECTIVE QUESTIONS

1. What kind of supervisory relationship do you seek with your supervisor?
2. What do you think are the defining characteristics of a good supervisory relationship?
3. What role, if any, do you think attachment patterns have in supervision?
4. What supervisor style do you prefer?

VIGNETTE 1

You are an experienced therapist and supervisee and have been attending Supervisor X on a weekly basis for the past three months. You have discussed your learning goals with the supervisor and want to focus on your case conceptualisation skills and treatment planning with a client who is presenting with complex trauma. However, your supervisor seems more focused on wanting you to process the impact of the work on your personal life and you are finding it frustrating. How might you address this with your supervisor?

VIGNETTE 2

As a newly qualified therapist, you have made an appointment with a new supervisor to meet for the first time. When you arrive at the supervisor's office, Supervisor Y is on the phone. You indicate that you will wait in the waiting room until the call is completed, but the supervisor beckons you into the room. It is clear that the conversation is of a personal nature and relates to the supervisor's adolescent child and lasts another ten minutes. The supervisor apologises for the delayed start and then begins to give you further details of the conversation and seeks your advice on how to address the issues with their adolescent. How do you react? How might you address the situation?

3

Supervision across the Career Lifespan

This chapter considers the supervisee experience from a professional and research perspective, and highlights some of the key issues in supervision across the career lifespan. It includes both trainee and experienced practitioner perspectives.

Supervision in the Context of Training

Embarking on counselling or psychotherapy training can be an arduous pursuit, from identifying a suitable course, applying for a place, being reviewed, often interviewed, to finally being offered a place on the course. Once they arrive on a course, beginning trainees have much to contend with in terms of new learning, not least of all becoming a supervisee. A myriad of relationships needs to be negotiated with course tutors, peers, supervisors and placement agencies, and, in many instances, it is the trainee's first experience of personal therapy. It may be a number of years since formal training or education has been undertaken or it may be the first time an individual has engaged in group learning.

One's own life context and the relationships within it may also need to be renegotiated to allow for full-time or part-time study. Personal and professional learning may also impact on those relationships (Mackenzie and Hamilton, 2007). Alongside this, a multitude of tasks needs to be accomplished with regard to course procedures, assignments, reading and so forth. Different methods of teaching and learning may be encountered for the first time. For example, experiential learning is a favoured approach on many training courses. For a trainee who is perhaps more familiar and comfortable with a didactic approach, an experiential learning approach, particularly in a group context, may be very challenging. Role-plays, presentations and video playback of skills sessions, while welcomed methods of learning, can be simultaneously experienced as anxiety provoking. However, experienced trainers and educators are usually very mindful of this – they were also trainees at some point! It is to be hoped that the trainee will be well supported in their learning. A good support system is an essential component in counselling and therapy training. I have heard the term 'an emotional rollercoaster' frequently applied to the initial training phase by the students with whom I work, and trainees at this developmental stage have much to take on board, including their role as a supervisee.

Supervision is considered by many to be a major training intervention with trainees in the helping professions (Folkes-Skinner et al., 2010). Along with academic course training and personal therapy, supervision is seen as a third element in the provision of therapist training (Rønnestad and Skovholt, 2001). This is clearly evident in training literature, with recurring declarations that supervision is an essential component in counselling and psychotherapy education (see, e.g., Milne and Oliver, 2000; Orlinsky and Rønnestad, 2005; Folkes-Skinner et al., 2010) and it is widely recognised as a professional activity (Goodyear et al., 2008). Clinical supervision, according to Shallcross and colleagues (2010: 503), 'is a central component in the training of graduate students in clinical, counseling, and school psychology', and Borders (2006: 70) has described supervision as 'a pivotal experience in the development of professional counselors'.

Supervision in counselling and psychotherapy is directly related to training in the pre-qualification phase and consequently inextricably linked to the training context. With reference to trainee counsellors, Howard and colleagues (2006), through the qualitative analysis of nine trainees' reflective journal entries, sought to understand the critical incidents experienced in trainee professional development during the first year of training. The authors identified five overarching themes that related to areas of 'professional identity, personal reactions, competence, supervision, and philosophy of counselling' (Howard et al., 2006: 88). With reference to supervision (which accounted for 10 per cent of the critical incidents reported), Howard et al. (2006) referred to both positive and negative experiences in supervision, and generally positive experiences in supervision were seen to promote confidence, insightfulness regarding client work and contributed to professional identity development. Not surprisingly, negative experiences contributed to a lack of satisfaction with supervision and the supervisor. The authors confirmed that experiences in supervision can either enhance or inhibit professional development.

A variety of themes are reported in the literature relating to supervision as making a positive contribution to professional development or, conversely and concerning, as a hindering factor. However, an important point to note here is that, in many of the supervision research studies emanating from the US, details of the training undertaken by the supervisor are rarely declared, which may or may not be a confounding variable. Nonetheless, supervision is acknowledged as a dominant influence in a trainee's personal and professional development and professional identity formation (Milne and Oliver, 2000). From their review of the literature, Gazzola and Theriault (2007: 190) reflect that 'Experienced practitioners who are considered "master therapists" frequently refer to the lingering impact of significant early supervisors on their counselling practice as well as on their wellbeing.' This is a profound responsibility for the supervisor and the profession.

Supervision for Clinical Placements in Training

For a trainee, the initial stages of training can be particularly challenging. This experience is most interestingly captured in a UK study aptly entitled '"A baptism of fire": a qualitative investigation of a trainee counsellor's experience at the start of training' (Folkes-Skinner et al., 2010). A trainee's professional development was charted over the first weeks of training and the trainee was interviewed at the beginning, middle and end of her first term. Findings from this case study indicate a number of revealing categories at these time points, namely:

1. 'Becoming something new – finding a way to be with future clients (Week 3)'.
2. 'Growth in therapeutic confidence through practice, role play experimentation, and reassuring supervision (Week 6)'.
3. 'Surviving "stressful involvement" through supervision that puts her pain into perspective, but doubts about her future as a therapist persist (Week 11)'. (Folkes-Skinner et al., 2010: 83)

This first category, 'becoming something new', referred to pre-practice preparation wherein the participant spoke about her feelings of uncertainty about meeting clients for the first time. Holding the client in mind was also a motivation to embrace her role as counsellor. Establishing good relationships with the course tutors was seen as helpful, together with a supportive supervisory relationship that helped the participant to normalise her concerns. As the participant/trainee gained some practical experience and felt scaffolded by supportive supervision, her confidence developed as related in the second category. By the end of the term, the participant trainee, while progressing tentatively, gains more balance in her perspective through effective supervision. In this case, the trainee's growing confidence is attributed largely to her experience of a supportive supervisory relationship which appeared to understand the stresses of training, particularly in the early stages of working with clients for the first time.

With reference to the placement experience, some similar features were found by Hill and colleagues (2007: 439–41) in their study of the challenges and gains in training for five trainees at the onset of their training. In this study, the following key experiences were identified:

Self-criticism: trainees reported concerns, anxiety and self-doubt regarding the challenge of meeting clients.

Reactions to clients: Feeling inadequate in relating to clients, expectations of client engagement in the therapeutic process and the challenge of staying within the boundaries of their professional role were cited as concerns.

Learning and using helping skills: and how best to apply these to facilitating their clients and concerns about getting it wrong.

Session management: participants reported the challenges of drop out, missed appointments and the pressure of accruing hours of experience. (2007: 439–41, italics in original)

In contrast, the gains reported related to 'feeling better about self as therapist' (2007: 9), with participants describing increased mastery of skills and decreased anxiety as they gained experience. They felt better 'able to connect with clients' (2007: 442) and became more comfortable in their role and more able to respond to what clients brought to therapy. Supervision was reported as a useful resource to contain trainee anxiety. Preference was stated for a supervisor who was directive, actively involved and clear about their expectations. High support and empowerment are required, particularly in the initial stages of training. Supervision can be a place where concerns are normalised and supervisees can be resourced.

Psychotherapy and counselling training is a unique learning environment whereby, in many theoretical orientations, the person of the therapist and their ability to engage in, maintain, evaluate and terminate effective therapeutic relationships are seen as paramount to positive therapy outcomes. Hence, the lines between personal and professional development can become blurred at times. For example, difficulties can frequently be seen as personal failures (De Stefano et al., 2007). The nature of the training experience may be experienced as stressful and anxiety provoking for the trainee (Folkes-Skinner et al., 2010).

As mentioned previously, supervision is inextricably linked to the training context for trainees, and the supervision experience will always be influenced by the contexts in which it occurs. Training courses in counselling and psychotherapy have different criteria relating to the clinical placement of trainees and different methods of contracting with placement agencies and with supervisors. Optimally, the training organisation collaboratively holds the management responsibility for placements, ideally provides placement opportunities for the trainee, and oversees the adequate provision of clinical supervision with appropriately qualified supervisors. Frequently, a contract is drawn up by the training course among the various stakeholders (i.e., trainee, supervisor, placement agency and training course) with criteria explicating the roles and responsibilities of each party for the provision of clinical placement opportunities for the trainee.

Most (though not all) training courses are accredited by a professional body (for example, the British Association for Counselling and Psychotherapy [BACP] or the British Psychological Society [BPS]) and specified criteria need to be met. For future individual accreditation/registration as a therapist, it is important that trainees are familiar with course and professional requirements from the outset. In addition to the course curriculum and personal therapy requirements (if relevant), clinical practice requirements usually include a stipulation of the number of client contact hours required overall and in relation to weekly caseload. The ratio of supervision hours to client hours, the frequency and mode of supervision, the professional identity and theoretical orientation of the supervisor and methods of evaluation in supervision may also be stipulated. It is also the norm to adopt the professional code of ethics of the accrediting body. The trainee has much information and logistical considerations to contend with in the initial stages of training before they ever meet a client or engage in formal supervision.

It is expected that, over the course of their training, trainees will have undertaken a variety of clinical experiences and will have worked with a range of clients. Again, depending on the nature of the training, a trainee may have multiple experiences of supervision and experience different supervisory styles. The supervisor may be internal to the placement agency or be an external supervisor. Some training courses (e.g., in individual therapy training) provide group supervision as an adjunct to individual supervision and in this instance a trainee may be working simultaneously with two supervisors. If a trainee has two concurrent placements, they may also have additional supervision requirements. In all cases, supervision needs to be held by clear contracts, with supervisor responsibilities delineated in relation to the clients under care (see Chapter 7).

On-site supervision can be very supportive of a beginning trainee and help them get to know the agency's procedures and the organisational culture in which they will be working. It is an important ethical consideration that clients who are referred to neophyte trainees have been screened as an appropriate referral for a trainee at their particular stage of clinical competence and for their theoretical orientation. In addition to duty-of-care responsibilities to the client, it can be very undermining of a trainee's confidence if they are referred a client whose therapy needs are beyond their competence. It is also advised that the supervisee discuss all potential onward referral of clients with their supervisor (Creaner, 2011b).

It is hoped that trainees will have positive experiences of supervision and, indeed, in their training. As a supervisor, I frequently ask about prior experiences of supervision when I meet with a new supervisee for the first time. In the majority of cases, the supervision experienced in training remains readily accessible to them and does, in my experience, have 'a lingering impact' as mentioned by Gazzola and Theriault (2007: 190). For the most part, their experiences in training were helpful rather than hindering. In these initial stages, supervision can be an oasis in the face of onerous training demands. The normative function of supervision (Proctor, 1987) can facilitate supervisees to make sense of the multiple contexts of the work, help keep focus on the individual needs of the client, which can sometimes, regrettably, get obscured in the policies and procedures of placement requirements.

Trainee Development in Supervision

As supervision in the training context facilitates professional development along with client welfare, therapist development is of central importance in supervision. There is an abundance of developmental theories that have been related to supervision (Hogan, 1964; Hill et al., 1981; Loganbill et al., 1982; Hess, 1987; Skovholt and Rønnestad, 1992; Williams et al., 1997). While many developmental approaches have been scrutinised with respect to their evidence base, the outcomes are ambiguous (Holloway, 1987; Ellis and Ladany, 1997). Developmental stage models may have more of an intuitive appeal than a solid empirical foundation (Bernard and Goodyear, 2009). In essence, developmental models propose that therapists move through various stages or phases (for example, from novice to master) in their acquisition of competence and as they gain experience.

Criteria regarding the learning outcomes for the knowledge, skills, attitudes and values that encompass personal and professional development in training should be detailed in the course curriculum and literature. Relevant assessment and evaluation procedures should also be detailed. It is important that supervisees are aware of how supervision fits into the overall picture of their training and how they will be assessed and evaluated in that regard.

With reference to the experienced practitioner, Page and Wosket (2001: 33) propose that as a 'learning perspective' is the focus of developmental models of supervision, 'consultation' is a more appropriate term for supervision in this regard, and such models have little relevance for the experienced practitioner. However, I suggest that the facilitation of learning is a key task of supervision across the career lifespan and agree that learning needs undoubtedly change as practitioners gain experience.

As previously mentioned, beginning trainees bring many questions to supervision, most notably: 'what is supervision?' A retrospective phenomenological study by Walker-Strong (2011) investigated the needs of trainees with six recent graduates of a two-year training course in counselling psychology. What was explicit in the findings was that trainees in the initial stages of training frequently did not know what supervision really entailed. 'What's it all about?' was a key question and theme as the majority of participants spoke of needing time to develop an understanding of what engaging in supervision meant in actual practice. Participants also recommended that specific induction be provided by a course prior to commencement of supervision. It was interesting to note that a number of areas needed clarification before the supervisee was ready to reflect on what they needed from supervision. For example, how to present client work in supervision, determining what was appropriate to bring to supervision and how to reflect on the work were key areas for clarification. As they gained experience, a shift in focus transpired whereby they moved beyond focusing on the technicalities of supervision and course requirements to a more self-directed perspective regarding how they could most productively use supervision for their professional development.

Post-training: Experienced Supervisee Perspectives

In the UK and Ireland, supervision is a mandated career-long requirement for practising counsellors and therapists who belong to the main professional bodies (for example, the BACP, the Irish Association for Counselling and Psychotherapy [IACP], and the United Kingdom Council for Psychotherapy [UKPC]). Few empirical studies have investigated the 'experienced practitioner as supervisee' perspective, particularly within the context of mandated supervision. In the US context, Usher and Borders (1993) conducted a survey ($n = 357$) of certified and experienced counsellors, seeking to investigate preferences for supervisory style and focus. In general, their results demonstrated a preference for a collegial relationship rather than a task-focused supervisory relationship among experienced practitioners. The preferred focus in supervision among this group pertained to 'conceptual, personalization, and process skills over professional skills and techniques' (Usher and Borders, 1993: 76).

In a European context, in a study by Weaks (2002) entitled 'Unlocking the secrets of "good supervision", the perceptions of nine experienced counsellors from Scotland and Ireland were sought. Participants came from different therapeutic orientations and contexts and were interviewed from the perspective of the supervisee. Employing a grounded theory approach, the supervisory relationship was identified as a core component of 'good supervision'. In addition, 'equality', 'safety' and 'challenge' were identified as core conditions for 'good' supervisory practice. While not a central focus of this study, supervisee style emerged as a pattern, and Weaks (2002: 37–8) identified four patterns of the experienced supervisee, namely:

1. *Affirmation seeking*: a good supervisory experience was evaluated in terms of how the supervisor treats the supervisee.
2. *Perfect practice seeking*: the good supervision experience in this instance was characterised by the supervisee feeling affirmed that they were adhering to best practice principles.
3. *Knowledge seeking*: when supervisees felt they were better prepared to move forward with alternative perspectives on process and practice, this was perceived as good supervision.
4. *Satisfaction seeking*: wherein the supervisee felt appropriately challenged, when both supervisor and supervisee were engaged in the process and the supervisee's 'high view of his/her complexity' was confirmed.

In contrast, Jacobs (2006) sought to identify the supervision needs and experiences of accredited counsellors and psychotherapists working in Ireland, where career-long supervision is also a professional requirement for counsellors and therapists. This study was a mixed method design ($n = 116$ self-report questionnaires) and seven semi-structured follow-up interviews were conducted. Regarding the key findings of participants' needs in relation to supervision, Jacobs (2006) discovered that 43 per cent of participants reported that 'supporting' is the most important need from the perspective of experienced practitioners/supervisees, with 88 per cent reporting that they always feel supported in supervision. Creating a learning relationship was identified by 27 per cent as the most important task. The barriers to having supervisory needs met were highlighted as the practitioners' own time constraints (20 per cent) and a lack of suitable (17 per cent) and available (13 per cent) supervisors. The participants in this research reported that issues of complaint procedures (66 per cent), legal issues (46 per cent), crisis procedures (31 per cent), supervisory relationship boundaries (33 per cent) and evaluation and feedback arrangements (31 per cent) were not adequately discussed or contracted for by their supervisors.

From an analysis of the accompanying seven semi-structured interviews, Jacobs (2006) found that the needs of supervisees related to a facilitative and equal relationship, process orientation to tasks, theoretical and ethical competence in the supervisor, a safe space for exploration, feedback and evaluation. Supervisor qualities that were identified were a sense of humour, collegiality and acceptance.

It is interesting, though not surprising, to note that equality and collegiality are recurring themes and are highly valued among experienced practitioners. Power differentials are not as pronounced as they are in training, and generally, though depending on work context, there is greater freedom of choice in selecting a supervisor. In addition, experienced supervisees may often have more specialist knowledge about their work context than their supervisor. For example, if the supervisee is working in the health service and the supervisor's context is private practice, the supervisee would have a greater knowledge of their work context. It is also interesting to note that psychological safety remains a need for experienced supervisees as well as trainees. While challenge was favoured by more experienced practitioners, support is generally identified as a trainee need before challenge is offered (Howard et al., 2006).

In a study that considered qualified psychologists' satisfaction with supervision and their confidence in providing supervision, McMahon and Errity (2013) surveyed 431 psychologists across diverse settings (health service, private practice and so forth) in Ireland. The findings reported that most psychologists typically attended supervision on a monthly basis with a little over half expressing satisfaction with their supervision. One third expressed dissatisfaction with supervision due in part to issues related to the supervisory relationship or the preferred focus of supervision. Again, psychological safety and trust in the supervisory relationship was identified as significant to a satisfactory supervision experience, with two-thirds of the respondents indicating that separation between line management and clinical supervision was preferable. Interestingly, McMahon and Errity (2013) reported that, while 70 per cent of the respondents provided supervision, only 16 per cent had undergone formal supervision training and 40 per cent felt confident in their supervisory role. Confidence in providing supervision was seen to be enhanced by experience and training.

The domains of supervision enquiry for experienced practitioners, as detailed by Page and Wosket (2001: 2), are generally focused on 'teasing out relationship dynamics, choosing among intervention options, dealing with feelings of frustration and boredom with clients, and considering how their personal and professional lives intertwine'. One's professional life does not proceed independently of one's personal life, and life events will become part of one's professional story. Staying renewed and healthy in the work is an ongoing area for reflection. The cumulative impact of the work, particularly for practitioners working in complex trauma and those who witness the extremes of human suffering, can be most challenging (see Chapter 9 for further discussion).

REFLECTIVE QUESTIONS

1. How have your supervision learning needs changed as you have gained experience as a therapist/counsellor?
2. How has your approach to supervision changed since your first supervision experience?
3. How do you stay healthy in the work while staying connected with clients?
4. What do you think and how do you feel about career-long supervision?

4

The Learning Landscape: Lifelong Learning in Supervision

This chapter reviews some of the key adult learning concepts as they pertain to learning in supervision. It also considers the means by which learning is best facilitated and the professional knowledge required for supervision practice.

Lifelong Learning

A career in therapy and counselling can be seen as a lifelong learning commitment. First coined by Faure et al. (1972), the concept of lifelong learning assumes that adults will continue to update their knowledge and skill in a continually and rapidly changing world. Competencies are time bound and require continual updating. As cautioned by Argyris and Schön (1974: 143), 'professional skills of yesterday and today will not be adequate in the future.' According to Skovholt and Jennings (2004: 9), 'the ordinary person must invest extraordinary amounts of time, practice, and commitment to develop expertise.' Maintaining and further developing that expertise also demands ongoing investment of multiple resources. This is acknowledged by many professional organisations in their continuing professional development (CPD) requirements, including supervision, as a condition of accredited or registered membership (for example, the British Association for Counselling and Psychotherapy [BACP] and the British Psychological Society [BPS]).

Lifelong learners are characterised by the following attributes, according to Candy and colleagues:

- an inquiring mind characterised by a love of learning, curiosity, a critical spirit, and self-monitoring of their own learning

- 'helicopter' vision involving mastery of a particular field paired with broad vision and a sense of the interconnectedness of different fields

- information literacy, including skill in locating, retrieving, decoding (from different sources, such as words, charts or diagrams), evaluating, managing and using information
- learning skills focused on 'deep' learning
- a sense of 'personal urgency' deriving from a favourable self-concept, self-organising skills, and a positive attitude to learning (1994: 43)

The task of the educator is to provide a learning environment that is facilitative of these aspects of the lifelong learner (Candy et al., 1994). As this pertains to supervision, the task of the supervisor is to encourage and support curiosity, critical reflection and self-evaluation; to help the supervisee apply and integrate relevant knowledge and skills; to promote 'deep' learning and the transfer of knowledge and skill to new situations; and to own their learning and developing expertise.

As with therapy and supervision, there is no one theory that can encapsulate how all adults learn. What we do have is an extensive set of theories and models that seek to explicate the adult learning process. Acknowledging the differences between how children learn and how adults learn, the concept of *andragogy* was posited by Knowles (1968). Andragogy focuses on how adults learn as opposed to *pedagogy* which, in general terms, focuses on what needs to be taught and the methods and strategies employed by the educator to achieve this. The concept of andragogy signalled a shift in perspective from the educator to the learner and subsequently learning perspectives took into account the contexts in which the learning occurs (see Merriam, 2008).

Knowles (1980) proposed that adult learners are self-governing and self-directed. As adults' frames of reference are the culmination of their life experience, information and knowledge, all of these aspects need to be related and integrated for learning to be meaningful. The starting point of adult learning is with the adult's experiences. Adult learners, according to Knowles (1980), have clear goals in mind when they embark on a learning journey and appreciate explicit learning goals, clearly defined objectives and a supportive, respectful learning environment in which these may be achieved. They also need to have a rationale for engaging in learning and value the pragmatics of usefulness to their personal and/or professional lives.

What Does this Mean for Supervision?

Conceptualising supervision as a learning relationship presupposes at a baseline level that learning will be facilitated, that the supervisee is a learner and that the supervisor is a facilitator of learning. Of course, the learning process is more complex than this, and adult learners also come to learning with a wealth of life experience and are 'knowers' as well as learners and supervisees. Supervisors are also knowers and learners, and supervision may be seen as a relationship that facilitates 'mutuality in learning' (Phillips and Kanter, 1984: 179).

Conceptualising supervision as a learning relationship also has implications for how learning is understood and how that learning is facilitated and evaluated. Traditionally, many supervisors who were not trained in learning theory and methodology largely drew on clinical approaches to achieve educational outcomes (Gregurek, 2007: 168). In recent years, with a growing emphasis on the need for dedicated training for supervisors, adult learning principles and strategies have been identified as a necessary component in many training curricula (Borders, 2009) and a core competence for supervisors (Falender et al., 2004).

Supervisee Learning Preferences

To facilitate a supervisee in a learning relationship, the supervisor needs to know how adults learn best, and supervisees also need to reflect on their learning needs, cognitive style and learning preferences. There are a number of resources (e.g., Honey and Mumford, 1982, 2000; Gardner, 1993), and the following may be useful for supervisee reflection in this regard. Derived from Kolb's experiential model, Honey and Mumford (1982) propose four primary styles of learning, namely that of 'reflector', 'theorist', 'activist' and 'pragmatist'.

1. *Reflectors* primarily learn through listening, are autonomous in learning and appreciate time to think things through and consider the topic of enquiry from multiple perspectives. Reflectors tend to resist task-orientated approaches, prefer to contribute to discussion when they have thought through implications and need time to consider.
2. *Theorists*, as the title reveals, enjoy ideas, facts, theories and concepts. They are engaged by problem-solving, questioning and discussion. They are also engaged by structured learning environments that facilitate logical exploration.
3. *Activists* are social learners and learn well in environments that generate discussion with others rather than lecture-style learning. They are active participants in learning, enjoy multiple learning methods and seek challenge.
4. *Pragmatists* are practical rather than theoretical in their approach. They are interested in the relevance of theory to practice and in finding new ways to do things. They prefer clear parameters in their work.

One of the challenges I encounter in considering learning styles inventories (e.g., Honey and Mumford's [1982] Learning Styles Questionnaire [LSQ)]; Kolb's (1976/1985) Learning Style Inventory [LSI]) is that they tend to be predictive in their assumptions and generally do not take into account personality factors and developmental or cultural variables (Cuthbert, 2005). In addition, with reference to both inventories named above, the psychometric properties remain controversial and tentative (Pickworth and Schoeman, 2000; Duff and Duffy, 2002; Cassidy, 2004). Counsellor and therapist education is also a unique context and less traditional in its teaching formats; hence, such inventories, while interesting to consider conceptually, may not be pragmatically useful in this environment. From an adult learning perspective, individuals and, in this case, supervisees learn in multiple and different ways at different times, and supervision needs to take this into account.

Experiential Learning

Experiential learning (Kolb, 1984) is recognised as a central model in clinical supervision to facilitate learning outcomes (Milne et al., 2008). In summary, this cognitive learning model comprises four stages in a learning cycle wherein, according to Kolb (1984: 38), *'learning is the process whereby knowledge is created through the transformation of experience'* (emphasis in original) rather than through instruction alone. Through this learning process, an experience is identified (*concrete experience*), intentionally reflected upon (*reflective observation*), theorised upon (*abstract conceptualisation*) and the theories generated are used to problem solve (*active experimentation*). One may commence on the learning cycle at any point, but one needs to proceed systematically through the next stages for learning to occur. The challenge is not to get stuck in any one stage. This learning cycle is the ground of reflective practice.

Reflective Practice in Supervision

Reflective practice has become something of a 'buzzword' in practice-based disciplines (for example, education, nursing, social work). Schön (1983), who coined the term, defines *reflective practice* as 'the capacity to reflect on action so as to engage in a process of continuous learning'. As therapists, we are trained to question our work continually, to formulate hypotheses and conceptualise theoretically what our clients present. We continually challenge and adjust those hypotheses as we get to know our client and as therapy progresses. We evaluate how progress is occurring on a moment-to-moment basis in the therapy session itself and afterwards in supervision as we critically reflect on that work and plan for the next session. We tease out what belongs to the client, to the therapist and what is co-constructed in the relationship. Naturally, we in the role of therapist bring our blind spots, preconceptions and biases to the work, and supervision provides a space where these can be reflected for our benefit as supervisees and for the benefit of our clients. Supervision and reflective practice are not synonymous, nor is the latter the prerogative of supervision. However, reflective practice should always be enabled within supervision (Fowler and Chevannes, 1998).

Supervision facilitates critical reflection on therapeutic practice through continual and deliberate reflection on all matters pertaining to professional practice and allows for connections to be made among these aspects (for example, the client, the supervisee, the organisation, the supervisory relationship). Engagement in 'reflection on action' can facilitate 'reflection in action' as supervisees gain experience and skill (Argyris and Schön, 1974) and begin to develop what Casement (1985) termed the 'internal supervisor'. Reflection in action and the 'internal supervisor' relate to the supervisee/therapist attending to the micro moment-to-moment experiences within the therapeutic relationship, the client, the person of the therapist, the interpersonal process between them – self-awareness in action. It is also framed by what the therapist knows in the context of a macro perspective of clinical assessment, research and clinically informed hypothesis, treatment planning, the norms of the profession and so forth.

Reflection on practice or reflective practice occurs after the fact in supervision. It values different forms of knowing and allows for integration of all the domains of professional knowledge. It can help us highlight discrepancies between our 'espoused theory' and 'theory in use' (our theory and how we apply it in practice) and therefore challenges new ways of thinking about a situation and new ways of responding to similar situations in the future. As suggested by Fook (2012: 45) from a social work perspective, 'the reflective approach recognises that theory is often implicit in the way professionals act and may or may not be congruent with the theory they believe themselves to be acting upon.' When such assumptions and pre-understandings are challenged in reflective practice, it can promote 'double-loop' learning, learning that expands habitual frames of reference. In other words, transformational learning can occur when we encounter a 'disorientating dilemma', a confusing event or situation that challenges our 'habits of mind', which requires a perceptual shift (Mezirow, 2000: 7).

Such reflection, both in and on practice, allows for increased self- and professional awareness, for learning from experience, for uncovering tacit knowledge (Polanyi, 1966), for transfer of that knowledge and for planning for future practice. Hence, as the self is constantly present in the reflective process, Fowler and Chevannes (1998) question the usefulness of reflective practice with beginning practitioners as they may not have the necessary skills or experience to engage in such a practice. They further comment that it may have a negative impact on the beginner and be frustrating for the learner. However, my experience as a supervisor has been contrary to this. While I agree that critical reflection skills need to be continually developed, frequently these skills are present through life experience, but may have become tacit for the trainee or not drawn upon initially in a new context. Helping a supervisee to make those skills explicit and apply them to the counselling situation is a task of supervision. Learning how to become a reflective practitioner takes time, skill and practice.

Developing Critical Reflection Skills in Supervision

There are many ways to reflect critically on practice: for example, through reflective writing, critical conversations with colleagues, critical incident analysis, systematically thinking through a situation or dilemma and so forth. 'Interpersonal process recall' (IPR; Kagan, 1980, 1984) is one such method that I have purposefully used and find helpful to facilitate critical reflection in supervision with the caveat that critical reflection is not about self-criticism, which would be counterproductive to the exercise. Furthermore, the focus is ultimately on the learning outcome for professional action rather than on the method of reflection.

Interpersonal Process Recall

Developed by Kagan in the 1960s (see Kagan, 1980, 1984), IPR has been applied to supervision as a method of increasing supervisee insight into their underlying thoughts and feelings as they relate to their interactions with clients (Cashwell, 1994). The IPR process involves the supervisor reviewing a video/DVD recording of a therapy session with the supervisee within a timeframe that adequately allows for optimal recall of the session. Ideally, the supervisee and supervisor decide and contract in advance on the focus of the session. For example, the supervisee could decide to look at critical incidents or significant events in the session. The supervisor then facilitates enquiry into the event by asking reflective questions for the purpose of heightening supervisee awareness. Bernard and Goodyear (2009) provide an extensive list of possible domains of enquiry and related questions that can be used in supervision to explore significant moments in session. For example, and depending on the focus of the supervision session and the event identified, the domains of enquiry could include, according to Bernard and Goodyear (2009: 230–1):

- *Leads that inspire affective exploration* (e.g., do you remember how you felt? What do those feelings mean to you?)
- *Leads that check out unstated agendas* (e.g., what would you have liked to say to her or him at this point? How were you feeling about your role as counsellor at this point?)
- *Leads that encourage cognitive examination* (e.g., what were you thinking at that time? What kind of image were you aware of projecting?)
- *Leads that get at images* (e.g., were any pictures, images or memories flashing through your mind then? Did it remind you of anything?)
- *Leads that explore mutual perceptions between client and counsellor* (e.g., what did you think she or he was feeling about you? Did you feel she or he had an expectation of you at that point?)
- *Leads that help search out expectations* (e.g., what did you want her or him to tell you? What did you really want to tell her or him at this point? What prevented you from doing so?).

Bernard and Goodyear (2009) offer a caution with IPR, suggesting that when discrete aspects of relationship dynamics are overly scrutinised, it may have the effect of misrepresenting the overall session. It is also important that a facilitative learning environment is established, particularly if IPR is used in group supervision. It is also important that sessions are reviewed in a timely fashion and as near as possible to the completed session to allow for optimal recall.

Professional Knowledge

The concept of 'professional knowledge', conceptualised by Eraut (1994), is useful to consider the knowledge and learning domains of supervision, together with a framework for guiding reflection on practice. Eraut (1994) refers to three main knowledge concepts within professional knowledge, all of which are relevant for the supervisee and for supervisors.

1. *Propositional knowledge* relates to theoretical and discipline-based knowledge or the 'knowing what' of professional activity. For supervisees, this relates to the knowledge base of psychological therapy, including theory and research. For the supervisor, this

relates to knowledge of both psychotherapy and supervision theory and the models and frameworks of each. Depending on theoretical orientation and the context in which supervision is provided, the supervisor may also draw on knowledge bases from a variety of other sources; for example, education, organisational psychology and so forth.

2. *Process knowledge* refers to 'know how' or procedural knowledge – knowing how to use propositional knowledge in a professional context. This is where theory is applied to practice for the supervisee. As this relates to psychotherapy supervision, the supervisor is in a parallel activity of applying the propositional knowledge of supervision to the supervisory process, while facilitating the supervisee to apply propositional knowledge of psychotherapy to the therapy process in order to develop their capability as practitioners and provide the best service to clients. 'Know how' may also draw on the personal knowledge and tacit resources of the supervisor.

3. *Personal knowledge* is derived from and informed by personal experience. As it may yet be tacit, it does not reach the explicit state of propositional knowledge. The concept of personal knowledge is expanded upon by Heron (1996: 33) who refers to 'experiential knowledge' as the knowledge gained from lived encounters with others, places and things and 'presentational knowledge', which makes explicit the tacit through symbolism, poetry and metaphor. The supervisor facilitates the therapist to make explicit their personal knowledge as it pertains to their client work. The symbolic and metaphorical are key resources in supervision. The parallel processes that may occur in supervision can also contribute to supervisee and supervisor awareness. The supervisor facilitates the supervisee to reflect upon their personal knowledge as it relates to the client. Optimally, the supervisor also engages in such reflection.

All professional development, according to Schön (1983), requires focus on propositional and professional knowledge. With reference to supervision, Bernard and Goodyear (2009: 4) propose that supervision 'provides the crucible in which supervisees can blend these two knowledge types and begin to incorporate them as their own working knowledge'. The blending of knowledge, from my clinical and training experience, is a unique endeavour for each individual supervisee as they draw on their personal knowledge. How this may be facilitated is the task of the supervisor in a collaborative learning relationship with the supervisee. The supervisee needs to be facilitated to blend the knowing 'what' of their discipline, the knowing 'how' to apply their knowledge, and the knowing 'why' they are doing it, so that they may embody their knowledge in a manner congruent with their professional identity and context.

The art and science of supervision is an intricate and complex interpersonal endeavour that draws on propositional, process and personal knowledge of both psychotherapy and supervision (Hewson, 2001). Professional knowledge or, in other words, theory and practice – the 'science' and 'art' of professional activity – are continually in dialogue with each other of necessity (Carr, 1995). Coles (2007) observed that the underpinning theories of our practice need to be explicated so that they may be fully understood. To achieve this, systematic reflection in and on practice needs to occur (Argyris and Schön, 1974). The questions of how learning occurs in supervision and how that learning is then transferred into therapy are pertinent areas of enquiry (Johnston and Milne, 2012).

REFLECTIVE QUESTIONS

Think of a client with whom you are currently working. As you reflect on your work with this client:

1. What knowledge is guiding your work?
2. What knowledge do you need to develop?
3. What skills are you using effectively?
4. What skills do you need to develop?
5. What attitude and values are you aware of in relation to this client?
6. If you were to apply a metaphor or an image to your work with this client, what would it be? What does it mean in relation to this client and the therapeutic relationship?
7. Have any 'disorientating dilemmas' arisen in your work with this client? How did you reflect on that? What was the outcome?
8. How can supervision best facilitate your learning for working with this client?

5

Models and Frameworks of Supervision

This chapter provides an introduction to some of the current supervision models and frameworks, as an example of how a supervisor might view a supervision session, and highlights areas of supervisor enquiry. An example of how a supervision framework may be used by the supervisee to prepare for and reflect upon their supervision session is discussed.

Models and Frameworks

A supervision model, according to Leddick (1994: 1), is 'the systematic manner in which supervision is applied'. As with the definitions of supervision, each model or framework focuses on particular aspects of supervision (Carroll, 1996). Many are formed on a particular worldview and understanding of the supervision relationship and process; and, again, while many are informed by research, few have been empirically tested (Milne, 2009). There is a wealth of research opportunity in supervision. While it is not possible to provide an account of the multitude of models and frameworks, I focus on a number that are in common use. I suggest that they can provide an orientation to the supervision process for supervisees, and consider how they may be a resource for maximising the supervision experience.

It may be somewhat curious to suggest that the neophyte supervisee should consider the models and frameworks of supervision, while simultaneously coming to terms with theories in counselling and psychotherapy. However, I do recommend that whatever developmental stage a supervisee is at, that they discover what supervision model or framework informs their supervisor's approach to supervision so that the supervisee can optimise their learning. In the same way that it is useful for the client to know about the therapeutic approach of their counsellor or therapist, it is useful for a supervisee to know how a supervisor approaches supervision. It is also a matter of informed consent. Understanding what supervision lens (and there are many lenses) through which a supervisor is viewing the work will help a supervisee become self-directed in their learning. The sample of supervision models and frameworks presented below is discussed as a means for supervisees to consider how best to use supervision.

Counselling Bound Models

In Chapter 1, we saw that supervision models were initially informed directly from developments in psychotherapy and counselling. There seem to be as many models and frameworks of supervision as there are definitions, but they can be categorised into two broad domains: those that arose directly from counselling and psychotherapy theories and those that have arisen from emerging supervision theory (Beinart, 2012). Generally, all counselling bound models seek to apply the principles of the therapeutic approach in a given orientation to the practice of supervision. According to Falender and Shafranske (2004: 9), 'theoretical orientation informs the observation and selection of clinical data for discussion in supervision as well as the meanings and relevance of those data.' For example, within the 'person-centred approach' (Rogers, 1951; Patterson, 1983), it is reasonable to assume that the person-centred supervisor will focus on facilitating the core conditions of empathy, positive regard, congruence and seeking psychological contact with their supervisees in order that the supervisee, in turn, will facilitate these conditions with their clients.

Therapy approaches have provided many concepts to the conceptualisation of supervision. For example, from the psychodynamic perspective, supervisor authority, internal supervisor, attachment behaviour, the working alliance, transference and counter-transference, and parallel process have been most pertinent to the development of supervision theory across perspectives (Bernard and Goodyear, 2009: 81).

One advantage of considering supervision within a therapy frame is that there is a body of theory and research to draw upon. Whilst supervision is a professional activity related to but distinct from therapy, concepts may not necessarily be transferable to supervision. Generic and supervision-specific models seek to address this. On the other hand, Davy (2002: 231) cautions that 'an overemphasis on generic models of clinical supervision may obscure ways in which the meaning of supervision and its possible practice is contingent on the specific setting in which it is conducted.'

Integrated Developmental Model

Developmental models, as mentioned in Chapter 3, seek to explain how therapist professional development occurs over the course of their training and, in some models, over the course of their careers. Originally developed in the 1980s by Stoltenberg (1981), the *integrated developmental model* (IDM) underwent further development by Stoltenberg and Delworth (1987) and was later revised by Stoltenberg, McNeill and Delworth (1998). The model describes four stages or developmental levels through which a trainee will progress on their journey from novice to expert. Accompanying these levels are three organising principles for evaluating professional development, namely: 'self–other awareness', 'motivation' and 'autonomy' across eight competency areas. These are (Stoltenberg et al., 1998: 187–8):

1. Intervention skills competence.
2. Assessment techniques.
3. Interpersonal assessment.
4. Client conceptualisation.
5. Individual differences.
6. Theoretical orientation.
7. Treatment goals and plans.
8. Professional ethics.

In summary, the four developmental levels as a follows:

> *Level 1: Self-centred*: This level is typified by high motivation on the part of the novice supervisee/trainee and the primary focus is on their own lack of competence. Little self-awareness is demonstrated, anxiety is high and supervisees appear dependent on the supervisor. The supervisee seeks structure and direction from the supervisor.
> *Level 2: Client-centred*: As supervisees begin to shift their focus from self to the client, they can oscillate between independence and dependence. At times, they can feel uncertain and ambivalent about their choice of career, particularly in the face of working with complex client presentations. The supervisee seeks support and modelling from the supervisor.
> *Level 3: Process-centred*: This level is categorised by more flexibility and the ability to focus on what is going on between self and the client. The supervisee seeks challenge from the supervisor.
> *Level 3i: Integrated – Process in context centred*: As confidence and competence develops, knowledge, insight, personal awareness and skills become integrated in the service of the client. High levels of self–other awareness are demonstrated along with high motivation and appropriate autonomy.

This is one of the few models that offer the supervisor suggestions for intervention at each of the levels to facilitate supervisee learning. For example, the authors recommend providing a structured environment, instruction which develops problem-solving skills and high support to contain supervisee anxiety. One of the difficulties with developmental stage models is that they tend to simplify trainee development and do not take factors such as cognitive complexity and the ability to integrate learning into account (Lochner and Melchert, 1997).

A Systems Approach

Holloway's (1995) comprehensive, research-informed *systems approach* to supervision encompasses a number of contextual factors (institution, agency and so on), supervision tasks and supervisor functions within the supervisory relationship, which comprises the structure of the relationship, the phases of the relationship and how the relationship is contracted. The process of supervision, according to Holloway (1995), is the dynamic interaction among the functions, tasks and the supervisory relationship as illustrated in Figure 5.1.

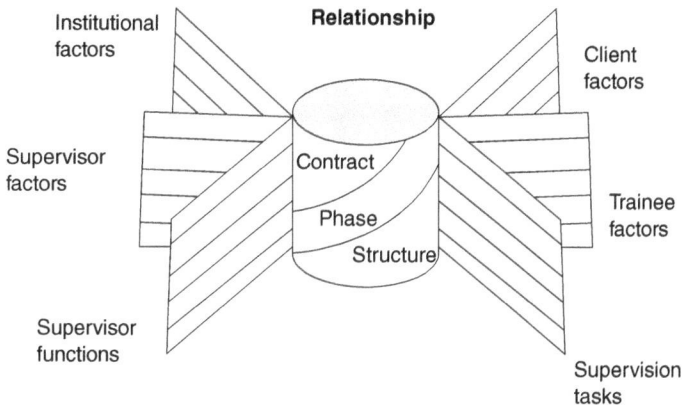

Figure 5.1 Holloway's (1995) systems approach to supervision.

Source: Holloway (1995: 58). Reprinted with the kind permission of Sage Publications.

Within this model, the tasks or competencies to be developed for the trainee/supervisee are:

- Counselling skill
- Case conceptualisation
- Professional role
- Emotional awareness
- Self-evaluation. (Holloway, 1995: 13)

To facilitate the supervisee to develop in these areas, the supervisor may be monitoring/evaluating, advising/instructing, modelling, consulting, supporting or sharing. For example, to facilitate the supervisee to develop their professional role and identity, the supervisor may select the function most relevant to the supervisee with reference to their developmental level, their learning needs in relation to a particular client, the nature of the client presentation and the context of the work. Holloway (1995) provides a process matrix (see Appendix 9) to demonstrate the interplay between supervision task and functions. It is a very systematic approach and the matrix can be used for tracking areas of focus. I find it particularly useful as a supervisor to see patterns of intervention with a supervisee.

Seven-eyed Process Model

Referred to by multiple names (the process model, the seven-eyed model, the double matrix model), this is a familiar model of supervision, in its various editions since 1989, and has a long tradition of use in the UK and Ireland. It presents a conceptual map to look at seven areas or modes in supervision. In this model, the supervisor is seen to take a 'helicopter view' of all the seven focal areas. According to Hawkins and Shohet (2012: 86), while supervision works at multiple levels simultaneously, supervision always involves five essentials elements, namely:

- a supervisor
- a supervisee
- a client
- a work context
- the wider systemic context

The process of supervision within this model is based on the double matrix of the client/supervisee and the supervisee/supervisor systems. The seven modes are focal points in supervision from which the supervisor chooses to focus upon in the supervision session (mediated by their particular style of supervision, the developmental level of the supervisee and relevant contextual factors). The authors recommend that supervisors need to be adept at using all modes to provide for effective supervision. Below are the modes or focal points of this model for the supervisor, as detailed by Hawkins and Shohet (2012: 85):

Mode 1: Focus on the client and what and how they present.
Mode 2: Exploration of the strategies and interventions used by the supervisee.
Mode 3: Focusing on the relationship between the client and the supervisee.
Mode 4: Focusing on the supervisee.
Mode 5: Focusing on the supervisory relationship.
Mode 6: The supervisor focusing on their own process.
Mode 7: Focusing on the wider context in which the work happens.

These modes are illustrated in the figure provided by Hawkins and Shohet (2012: 87), with the first three modes focusing on and exploring what happens in the supervisee/therapist–client session (see Figure 5.2). The focus of the next three modes is on the supervision session itself and how this is experienced by the supervisor and supervisee within the supervisory relationship, which may also be influenced by the dynamics of the supervisee/therapist–client relationship (see 'parallel process' in Chapter 2). Supervisor self-awareness is highlighted in Mode 6, with Mode 6a in Figure 5.2 referring to the 'fantasy relationship between the client and the supervisor' (Hawkins and Shohet, 2012: 96). This relationship may be considered as 'fantasy' as the supervisor has never met the client and relies on the supervisee to communicate (consciously and unconsciously) information regarding the client. The final mode provides a lens to the variety of contexts that may influence the work of therapy and supervision.

This model also takes into account the developmental stage of the supervisee, their theoretical orientation, the contract and the setting of the work. Scaife (2001: 71)

Organisational context

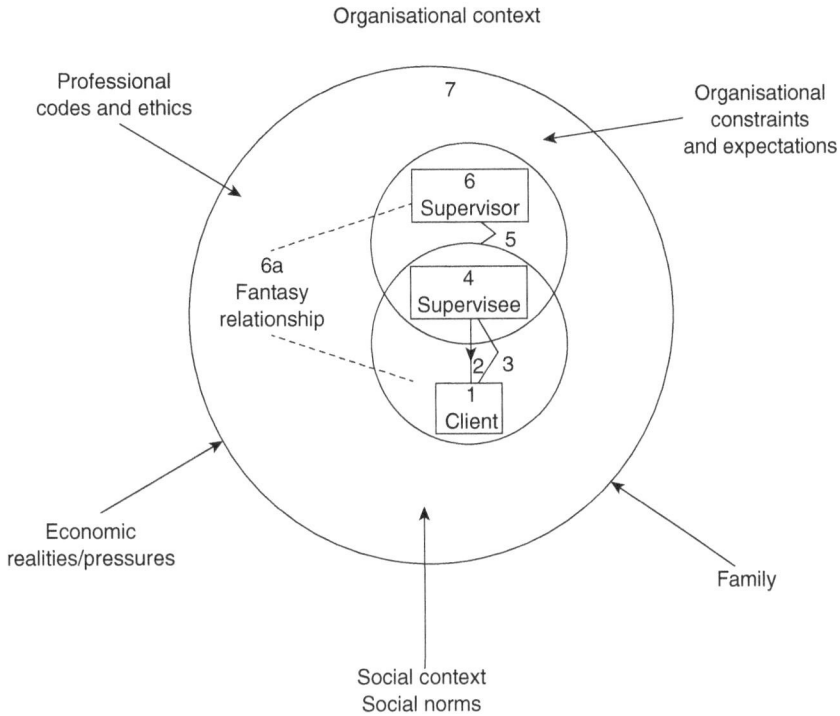

Figure 5.2 The seven-eyed model of supervision (Hawkins and Shohet, 2012).

observes that this model asks the question 'what are my experiences in supervision telling me about the work?' The supervisor, using their own process and competency, facilitates the supervisee to deepen their awareness of their internal processes and the external factors influencing their work.

One way in which I use this model with supervisees is in a group supervision format to provide training in using a supervision model and as a framework to prepare for supervision. It would be used and contracted for (see Chapter 7) with an established group of more experienced supervisees, rather than beginning trainees, whereby group members become co-supervisors. For example, in a group of eight, and drawing on the format of a reflective team (Prest et al., 1990), one supervisee presents their client work for supervision and each of the other supervisees takes responsibility to track one of the seven modes. At the end of the session, each supervisee shares two observations or questions they have with respect to their focus area. Within this model, typically, not all of the modes would be reviewed or, indeed, be relevant in every supervision session, and focusing too broadly would diminish the depth of the work for the supervisee presenting and for the group. Furthermore, the supervisee could feel overwhelmed with so much feedback on a continual basis. However, for the purpose of this exercise, and by using the model in this manner, supervisees report that it broadens their perspective on supervision as it provides a framework from which to reflect on their client work, prepare for supervision and provide feedback to other group members. Once they become familiar with the model, or any model for that matter, they may select the mode or modes which they feel are most relevant to the particular presentation. Nevertheless, the supervisor would hold an overview of all the modes of enquiry.

Generic Tasks of Supervision

Carroll's (1996) *generic tasks model* emerged from his research with supervisees and supervisors from which seven tasks of supervision were identified. These tasks speak to what the supervisor 'does' in supervision and how supervisors behaviourally implement their role. From a supervisee perspective, this model provides a very useful framework for use in supervision, acknowledging that the supervisor is responsible for implementing the tasks (Figure 5.3).

In working with new supervisees, I frequently draw upon this framework to assist them in preparing for supervision and to guide evaluation of their supervision session. For example, in Table 5.1, Carroll's generic tasks are listed and, drawing on this model, I have provided sample questions for supervisee reflection to help them identify their learning needs, prepare for a supervision session and evaluate their learning and supervision experience.

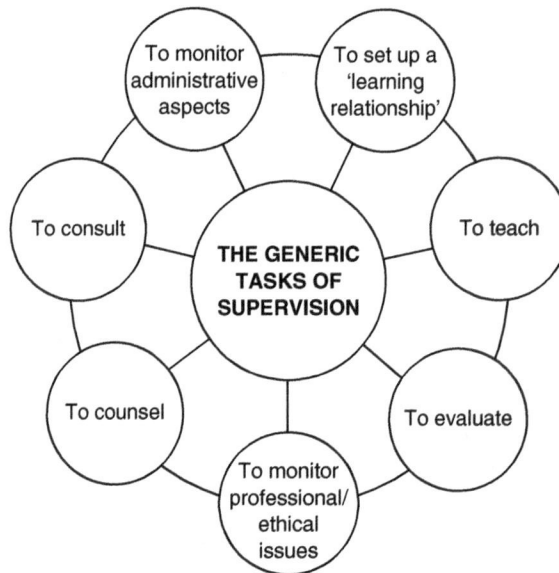

Figure 5.3 Overview of the seven tasks of supervision in Carroll's (1996) generic tasks model.

Source: Carroll (1996: 53). Copyright © M. Carroll 1996. Reprinted with the kind permission of Sage Publications.

Table 5.1 Carroll's (1996) generic tasks of supervision with sample questions for reflection

Carroll's generic tasks	Supervision preparation questions for the supervisee *With reference to your developmental level, consider the following questions*	Evaluation of supervision questions
1. Creating the learning relationship	What kind of supervision relationship do you want? What tasks, goals and emotional bond do you want to establish in your supervision relationship? How are you contributing to the supervision relationship? How are you engaging in supervision?	How has the supervision relationship been contracted? How are you experiencing your supervision relationship? Your supervisor's style?
2. The teaching task	What are your learning needs for this session? What knowledge do you need to develop? What skills do you need to develop? What attitudes/beliefs are relevant?	How do you think that your learning has been facilitated in this session? What was your key learning?
3. The counselling task	Are you aware of any personal biases, assumptions, experiences that are pertinent to your work with the client(s) you are presenting in supervision? What personal issues related to client work might you bring to supervision? What personal issues related to client work might you bring to your personal therapy?	How comfortable do you feel about bringing personal information as it relates to your client work to supervision? How is it processed by your supervisor?
4. Monitoring professional/ethical issues	What professional issues are relevant to your client work at present? What ethical issues or dilemmas are emerging?	How well do you think your professional/ethical issues have been discussed in supervision? How does your supervisor monitor these issues?
5. The evaluating task	How are you self-evaluating your strengths as a therapist with this client(s)? What areas for development are emerging? What resources do you need to develop these?	How is supervision helping you to balance your self-evaluation? What is your supervisor evaluating? How are they evaluating? What opportunities do you have to provide evaluation of your supervision experience with your supervisor?

(Continued)

Table 5.1 (Continued)

Carroll's generic tasks	Supervision preparation questions for the supervisee *With reference to your developmental level, consider the following questions*	Evaluation of supervision questions
6. The consultative task	Consider all of the relationships that influence your client work: how is each pertinent to your work with this client? Supervision relationship? Therapeutic relationship? Transferential/counter-transferential relationship?	What is your experience of your supervisor's consultant role?
7. The administrative task	How are the organisational contexts in which you work influencing your work with this client? What other contexts are relevant to your client work?	How are these contexts addressed in supervision? How are these contexts influencing your supervision experience?

Source: Adapted from Carroll (1996: 56).

Best Evidence Synthesis Model

Conceptual frameworks can help us to reflect on core concepts and provide structure to complex processes. However, they fall short of explicating theory. Some models of supervision are highly complex and complicated to navigate, while others are too simplistic to hold the intricacies of the supervisory process. Few models have been tested and empirical support is yet to be determined (Milne et al., 2008). However, while it is useful to consider that no one model can ever hold the complexity of human nature and behaviour, we need to establish the 'what' of supervision to best inform the 'how' of supervision, in an effort to find the 'Goldilocks' model. The main issues that exist with many of the models to date are well summarised by Milne et al. (2008: 172) when they state: 'The majority of clinical supervision models and theories are untested and not grounded in the empirical literature, most empirical investigations do not explicate and test supervision theory, and much of the extant empirical literature lacks conceptual-methodological rigor.'

In an attempt to address this deficit, Milne et al. (2008) conducted an empirical review of 24 supervision research studies to produce a *best evidence synthesis* (BES) basic model of supervision with a view to developing this further. The results of this review reported 32 contextual variables of successful supervision, 26 supervision interventions and 28 outcomes of effective supervision identified to form the BES model. Of the 32 contextual variables reported, organisational context, client/patient, supervisee and supervisor factors, learning factors and research factors were seen to moderate the effects of supervision (Milne et al., 2008: 178). With reference to the supervision interventions identified to facilitate supervisee learning, teaching and instruction were identified in three-quarters of the studies, with corrective feedback, observation of the supervisee's work, and goal-setting interventions being the highest ranked. The outcomes identified related to changes in 'supervisee attitudes, increased emotional self-awareness, changes in supervisees' motivation, and improved skills' (Milne et al., 2008: 180). The authors note that Kolb's (1984) 'experiential learning cycle' was evident in supervisee learning outcomes and that experiential learning was identified as significant in the studies reviewed.

REFLECTIVE QUESTIONS

Think of a client with whom you are working. Drawing on Holloway's (1995) supervision tasks, consider the following questions:

- *Counselling skill*

  - What counselling skills, interventions and strategies are helpful with this client?
  - Which ones are not/have not been helpful? How so?
  - What counselling skills are you most comfortable with and confident in using?
  - Which ones require some further development?

- *Case conceptualisation*

  - How do you theoretically describe your client's concerns?
  - How do you clinically understand your client's presenting problem and concerns?
  - What informs this? What evidence is available to support this?
  - What does your conceptualisation mean in terms of helping your client address their concerns?
  - What support and resources are available to you and to the client?

- *Professional role*

  - What are you learning about your professional role from this client in this context?
  - Are there any potential challenges to your professional role?
  - Are there any potential ethical or legal issues for consideration?
  - How are you documenting your work with this client?

- *Emotional awareness*

  - How is working with this client impacting upon you?
  - What thoughts, reactions and emotional responses does your client evoke in you? How so?

(Continued)

(Continued)

- *Self-evaluation*

    o What are your areas of strength in your work with this client?
    o What are areas for development and resourcing in relation to knowledge, skills and attitudes/values as you consider this client and your work together?
    o How can supervision help you further reflect upon the questions raised above?

6

Forms and Formats of Supervision

This chapter presents an overview of group, peer and live supervision, and considers the use of technology in supervision with reference to online supervision.

Group Supervision

Many models of supervision generally refer to individual supervision with other modalities, if included, discussed as an extension of the individual model (Starling and Baker, 2000). Until quite recently, few texts dedicated specifically to group supervision were to be found (see, for example, Proctor, 2008). While the predominant and generally preferred format of supervision is the supervisor/supervisee dyad, group supervision can be a valuable adjunct to training or as a format in its own right.

Group supervision has been defined by Bernard and Goodyear (2009: 244) as:

the regular meeting of a group of supervisees (a) with a designated supervisor or supervisors, (b) to monitor the quality of their work, and (c) to further their understanding of themselves as clinicians, of the clients with whom they work, and of service delivery in general. These supervisees are aided in achieving these goals by their supervisor(s) and by their feedback from and interactions with each other.

From the literature, it appears that there is much variation in what constitutes group supervision, with group size, content and focus in the session, time spent processing group dynamics, length of session and experience and training of the supervisor being noted variables (Riva and Cornish, 1995; Riva and Erickson Cornish, 2008).

While little research exists on the efficacy of group supervision, many advantages and disadvantages of this format have been outlined (Enyedy et al., 2003; Linton and Hedstrom, 2006). On the positive side, group supervision is seen as providing a rich learning environment, as multiple peer perspectives are available to the supervisee, with a greater range of client issues being made available for discussion and reflection

(Baruch, 2009). Vicarious learning can occur for the supervisee in hearing feedback provided to peers, in providing feedback to a variety of practice contexts, and in receiving feedback from different perspectives, all of which 'maximise the resources of a group practice' (Russell-Chapin and Chapin, 2012: 136). It is also suggested that group supervision has an efficiency of time and economic advantage (Hawkins and Shohet, 2012: 177).

With reference to the potential disadvantages of group supervision, Glickauf-Hughes and Campbell (1991: 626) outline the following dynamics that may interfere with the learning process:

1. Competition among supervisees.
2. Increased feelings of shame.
3. Increased defensiveness of the supervisee presenting a case.
4. Interference with the supervision process by other group members.
5. Non-facilitative group norms.
6. Differential abilities among group members.

In considering hindering events that interfered with learning in group supervision experiences among counselling and counselling psychology trainees ($n = 49$), Enyedy et al. (2003: 312) identified 61 such events which were then clustered into five overarching phenomena, namely:

1. *Between-member problems*: Experiences in this cluster related to negative supervisee behaviours; for example, competition among group members, varying levels of investment and motivation to participate fully in group supervision.
2. *Problems with supervisors*: Some of the examples in this category identified negative supervisor behaviours; for example, the supervisor dominating the time, being over-critical or not having adequate experience, expertise or clinical focus and over-focusing on administrative issues.
3. *Supervisee anxiety and other perceived negative affects*: In this cluster, a number of anxieties were identified by the participants, which included anxiety arising from peers listening to a taped session or from not being prepared for supervision, fear of evaluation, being in a minority in the group (e.g., being the only male), feeling unsafe, feeling under pressure to disclose and being more sensitive to group feedback.
4. *Logistical constraints*: The timing of supervision, the absence of the primary supervisor, room size and a lack of variety in case presentation were the experiences highlighted in this regard.
5. *Poor group time management*: In this cluster, lack of time to present/discuss cases/time management and group size were the main experiences named as hindering learning in group supervision.

It was interesting that the cluster entitled 'Problems with supervisors' was the largest category, with 24 hindering phenomena being identified. From this category, Enyedy et al. (2003) provide clear recommendations for supervisors undertaking group supervision. In summary, they recommend that supervisors are sufficiently trained and experienced to undertake the group supervisor role, with knowledge and skill relating to developmental changes in supervisees and with the ability to stay focused on the issues presented.

They suggest that feedback is provided in a direct, but not overly critical manner, and that boundaries regarding confidentiality are explicit. The group supervisor is advised to respect the theoretical orientation of the supervisee, particularly if it differs from that of the supervisor. To maximise learning, the authors recommend that the group supervisor avoid engaging in power struggles with supervisees and manage conflicts within the group as they arise. In the latter, when the conflict is between the supervisor and supervisee, supervisors are encouraged to respond proactively and non-defensively to the supervisee.

In relation to recommendations to group supervisees, Enyedy et al. (2003: 315) suggest that:

Supervisees should also take an active role in their learning process by being clear with their supervisor about their training needs and by engaging in discussions with their group supervisor regarding the supervision process and how to improve it. Although it may be difficult to provide honest and direct feedback to a supervisor when there are problems with the supervision group, this feedback is an important component of the success of the group supervision experience.

In developing their grounded theory model of group supervision processes, Fleming and colleagues (2010: 198) reported similar issues and also provide recommendations regarding group supervision. Not surprisingly, the authors discovered that psychological safety was a central construct which optimised learning for group supervisees. When supervisees felt safe, they behaved in an open and receptive manner and this contributed to group safety and learning. Conversely, when they felt unsafe, this mitigated others feeling safe and overall learning was diminished. Factors that hindered learning related to physical/environmental problems (e.g., feeling unwell, working in a cold room); an absent peer; distraction (e.g., supervisee dealing with personal issues and not engaged in supervision); and time constraints (e.g., too much time with too few clients or too little time with too many clients). Unresolved conflicts, defensiveness and intense anxiety as experienced by supervisees were also reported as hindering events. Factors that contributed to safety included both individual (openness to supervision/being able to be vulnerable) and group factors (group cohesion, fluid leadership and discussion of group processes).

According to Baruch (2009), in addition to the skills required for individual supervision, group supervisors need to have a very good understanding of group processes, dynamics and management, and hold effective leadership, evaluative and administrative skills in this context. In their systematic review of 11 studies that explored supervisees' experiences and perceptions of group supervision, Mastoras and Andrews (2011) provide clear recommendations for group supervision practice. While highlighting the methodological issues that are apparent in many of the available studies, the authors present a number of themes that were clearly apparent across cases. The importance of peer feedback was identified as a predominant theme, and the authors recommend that group supervisors actively encourage, moderate and facilitate peer feedback among group participants rather than offering individual supervision in a group context, while at the same time providing input, feedback and support. Supervisor flexibility in balancing the multiple roles of the group supervisor was encouraged, and the importance of time management was again highlighted as an essential supervisor skill. The majority of studies reviewed referred to the supervisor needing to manage group process and dynamics, particularly in relation to promoting group cohesion and safety and managing conflicts. Frequent opportunities for formative feedback and open discussion were indicated, and adopting a developmental perspective was promoted. Supervisee anxiety, which may be considered as normative in beginning supervisees, was also highlighted as an area that needed attention and required management by the supervisor. In this regard, the explicit discussion of anxiety was recommended in the beginning stages of the group to normalise supervisees' feelings. Supervisors were encouraged to facilitate supervisees to reframe anxiety as an opportunity for personal development and openly discuss helpful coping strategies.

Peer Supervision

Peer supervision is widely practised by post-qualification therapists and, in some instances, as an adjunct to training. Peer supervision comes in many shapes and sizes (dyadic, triadic or group) and can be a useful means to facilitate reflection on practice and provide support for the practitioner. It can be a cost-effective method of supervision for supervisees. Wilkerson (2006: 62) defines peer supervision in the following terms:

> Peer supervision is a structured, supportive process in which counselor colleagues (or trainees), in pairs or in groups, use their professional knowledge and relationship expertise to monitor practice and effectiveness on a regular basis for the purpose of improving specific counseling, conceptualization, and theoretical skills.

The emphasis here is that peer supervision is a planned and structured collegial professional relationship that focuses on competence development and the monitoring of best practice. One of the challenges of peer supervision is that it can lack challenge and be excessively supportive (Borders, 1991).

Live Supervision

Emanating from family therapy, live supervision is now widely practised among mental health professionals and in training programmes (Champe and Kleist, 2003). In essence, live supervision constitutes the supervisor being actively present throughout a session between practitioner and client. This may be conducted via a two-way mirror, with the supervisor providing feedback to the therapist through a 'bug in the ear' or 'phone-in' method. Alternatively, the supervisor may be present in the therapy room intervening as required. Interestingly, as one might presuppose, research demonstrates that interruptions to the therapist, if not too numerous and if conducted in a collaborative manner for which a clear contract exists, do not adversely affect the therapeutic process or impact negatively on therapist/supervisee anxiety (Champe and Kleist, 2003).

Online Supervision

Rapid developments in technology over the past decades have had a profound effect on global and interpersonal communication and no less so on supervision and therapy practice (Anthony et al., 2010). While the use of technology in supervision is not new (e.g., audio/visual recording, 'bug in the ear'), recent developments are noticeable in the terminology applied to supervision (e.g., cyber-supervision, online supervision, web conferencing supervision). The advantages of using online communication in supervision include accessibility, particularly in rural locations where access to supervision may be limited, and reduced travel costs (Olson et al., 2001).

Online supervision can be delivered in a number of ways: for example, in real time (synchronous) via web-based video conferencing, instant messaging or Internet relay chat (IRC) groups, or via time-delayed methods (asynchronous), typically email and list servers.

All of the forms that are available face to face (individual, group, peer) are also available virtually, with the notable difference that supervisor and supervisee do not need to be in the same physical space. Online supervision can be text based (e.g., email) or may employ a web camera whereby the supervisor and supervisee/s can see and hear each other via their computers and the Internet (e.g., Skype).

Some of the disadvantages of online supervision frequently cited are the lack of non-verbal cues associated with talk-based supervision, the possibility of misunderstandings and the potential implications for developing an optimal supervisory relationship (Vaccaro and Lambie, 2007). Research in this area is in its infancy and few empirical claims can be currently made. Nonetheless, in a study that compared online (voice-based) and face-to-face group supervision with trainees, Nelson and colleagues (2010) found no differences in satisfaction levels between the two groups. Similarly, in a comparison between two online supervision conditions (one text-based and one text and video), both formats were found to be equally effective (Coker et al., 2002).

Along with the professional and ethical considerations that apply to all supervisory and therapy practices (see Chapter 7), a number of practical issues are present in online supervision for both the supervisor and supervisee, and these need to be included in the initial supervision contract. Anthony and Goss (2009: 10–11) outline key areas for agreement between the supervisee and supervisor, specifically:

- Agreement regarding the mode of communication, taking into account geographical locations and differences in time zones.
- Asynchronous modes of communication need to be secure, password protected and encrypted and ensuring such security rests with each user.
- Agreement regarding a contingency plan in the event of a technical failure.

Issues of confidentiality, privacy and informed consent are always key factors in therapy and supervision, and are particularly so in online work. Documentation and security of records are also pertinent areas for supervision discussion in this context. Online supervision, along with online therapy, is considered a specialist area and requires specific training. Please see Chapter 9 for further discussion of some of these areas.

REFLECTIVE QUESTIONS

1. What do you see as the advantages/disadvantages of individual supervision versus group supervision?
2. What do you see as the benefits and challenges of online supervision for you?
3. What technological security issues need to be considered in online supervision?
4. What is your preferred supervision format? Why?

Beginning the Learning Relationship

This chapter will develop the perspective of the supervisory relationship as a learning relationship within both a training and post-training context. It considers the professional boundaries that are necessary to establish and maintain a supervision relationship. It provides guidelines for developing a learning agreement with a supervisor with reference to individual supervisee contexts.

Establishing Boundaries in Supervision

Boundaries are needed for any relationship to grow and develop. We know from systems theory and family therapy that rigid and inflexible boundaries in family relationships inhibit the growth of individuals within the family system. We also know that having few or overly permeable boundaries can cause confusion, feelings of insecurity and a lack of safety in the family context.

In the context of therapy, while mediated by theoretical, social and cultural phenomena, there is also general agreement that professional boundaries are required for client protection in the therapeutic relationship (Luchner et al., 2008). The establishment and maintenance of appropriate boundaries are clearly promoted in the professional codes of ethics to which helping practitioners subscribe and apply to all professional practice. In relation to supervision specifically, multiple professional boundaries are optimally established in the contract and in the practice of supervision. These define the roles of the supervisor and supervisee working together in a professional relationship (Power, 2007) and also differentiate supervision from other professional activities. Carroll (2007: 36) encapsulates the boundary essence of supervision when he states that: 'There is no such thing as supervision where work is not reviewed, interviewed, questioned, considered and critically reflected upon. Supervision that is not centred and focused on actual practice and work is simply another form of counselling or psychotherapy.'

One of the difficulties that can arise in supervision, particularly psychotherapy supervision, is that the lines between therapy and supervision can become blurred. As recounted by Rubin (1989: 395), 'I speak and hear often how supervision is not therapy. That is not in dispute. Yet it may not always be helpful or necessary to dichotomise our listening and intervention skills in the therapeutic and supervision situations.' Supervision can have a therapeutic value to the supervisee and may be a catalyst for them to seek therapy (Page and Wosket, 2001). However, supervision clearly holds a gatekeeping function and, as such, effects an evaluative role highlighting the power differential, and consequently a boundary needs to be held between supervision and therapy in the interests of the supervisee (Whiston and Emerson, 1989).

This begs the question of the 'restorative' (Inskipp and Proctor, 1995) and 'reparative' (Gilbert and Evans, 2000) dimensions of supervision and whether they need to be considered as welcomed consequences of a good supervision relationship or functions to be effected within supervision. In the context of supervision in nursing, Yegdich (1999: 1267) offers the following distinction: 'therapy changes the patient's mode of reacting to enable effective functioning, while supervision teaches the supervisee psychotherapeutic skills.'

While supervisees express a desire for their personal concerns to be brought to supervision (Shanfield et al., 1993, 2001), the issue remains unresolved in the literature. It is an issue that also pertains to the training of psychotherapy and supervision trainees. Personally, I am mindful of the dual role possibility and the ethical implications of that. I also see a necessary place in supervision for the personal feelings, thoughts and reactions of the supervisee to the client to be welcomed as knowledge in use to be reflected upon from a supervision perspective. Part of the role of the supervisor is about facilitating the supervisee to distinguish between 'what belongs to them', which then may be brought to therapy or other personal development settings, and what has emerged from their engagement in the therapeutic relationship or the supervisory relationship. As Page and Wosket (2001) contend, there needs to be sufficient safety in the supervisory relationship for supervisees to disclose whatever is impacting upon their client work. They further suggest that it is the responsibility of the supervisor to manage the boundary between supervision and therapy, whilst 'the supervisor can legitimately listen to and acknowledge the personal distress of a supervisee without slipping into therapy' (Page and Wosket, 2001: 51).

From my perspective, while supervision may be experienced as therapeutic, the goal is not therapy. The focus needs to remain on the client work and reflection on that practice in the context of supervisee development and the welfare of the client (Carroll, 2007). Conceptualising supervision as a learning relationship may help mitigate such boundary issues and keep the defining feature of supervision – namely, evaluation – to the foreground.

Clinical Supervision and Line Management

The idea of supervision being conceived of as Burton (1930: 1046) originally described, 'snoopervision' or 'detective work', is less prevalent in the supervision of private practice work with an external supervisor than in an organisational context whereby line management supervision and clinical supervision may be insufficiently differentiated (Copeland, 1998).

Many policy documents and guidelines clearly distinguish between clinical supervision and line management or managerial supervision (e.g., BPS, 2007) and it is similarly distinguished in supervision literature (e.g., Carroll, 2001; Cutcliffe et al., 2001; Kavanagh et al., 2002). However, some of the quality assurance responsibilities of both managerial and clinical supervisor can look similar (monitoring best service to clients, caseload review, working within organisational structures, good practice in record keeping and so forth). One of the key differences in the role of line manager is that they may be involved in organisational performance reviews for disciplinary reasons or for career promotion.

Defining Boundaries

Power (2007) suggests that boundaries are essential to the integrity of supervision. While it is the supervisor's responsibility to manage these boundaries, the supervisee also needs to be involved in negotiating them. Power (2007: 55–6) proposes that the following boundary areas need to be negotiated and established within a supervision relationship:

1. *The boundary of relationship*: this boundary has a dual aspect, one with reference to establishing a relationship and the second with reference to establishing a professional relationship in supervision that is distinguished from a therapeutic relationship. Dual relationships also need to be discussed.
2. *The boundary of content*: this refers to negotiation on what will be discussed in supervision within the parameters of that which pertains to the work.
3. *The boundary of time*: the frequency and length of supervision sessions and the duration of the supervision contract are clarified.
4. *The boundary of space*: the location, the supervision environment and ensuring privacy are established.
5. *The boundary of confidentiality*: the parameters of confidentiality, including the limits of confidentiality, need to be discussed as they pertain to the supervisee and the client(s). Administrative record keeping is also discussed.

Getting to Know your Supervisor

The boundary of the supervisory relationship, as discussed earlier, is central to good supervision outcomes. It takes time for a supervisee and supervisor to get to know each other. Both parties need to make certain aspects of the supervisory process explicit in order to work effectively together. From the perspective of the supervisee, it is reasonable to know the theoretical orientation of the supervisor both as a therapist and a supervisor. It is also appropriate that the supervisee knows the supervisor's qualifications, experience and particular expertise, again as both therapist and supervisor.

From a supervisor's perspective, they will want to know the supervisee's professional background, theoretical orientation, training, experience and the organisational contexts of the work. The style of supervision being sought and previous experiences in supervision are also relevant. In the case of the supervisee being a trainee, the organisational contexts will refer to both the training course and the placement agency.

Interestingly, Lidmila (1997) notes that the supervisor's need to know may be motivated by anxiety, which may in turn contribute to supervisee anxiety and call forth defensiveness and concealment. From this psychodynamic perspective, the supervisee's experience of 'not knowing' may contribute to experiences of shame, splitting, projective identification, idealisation, avoidance and withdrawal. Lidmila (1997: 40) refers to three shame-provoking modes of enquiry that may be employed by the supervisor as they seek to know: 'the detective', 'the inquisitorial' and 'the librarian'. The supervision encounter may also activate feelings of shame in the supervisor, around their 'not knowing' and competence as they attempt to balance their multiples roles and responsibilities (Hahn, 2001). The mode of enquiry recommended by Lidmila (1997: 44) for the supervisor is that of 'travelling curiously without a guide' but with some reference points for the journey.

Implementing Boundaries and Beginning Supervision

Contracting has become a widely used activity in supervision, and detailed guidelines for the contents of these are available (e. g., Carroll, 1996; Sutter et al., 2002; Hawkins and Shohet, 2012). Contracts can make explicit the roles, responsibilities, rights and relationship for the supervision experience and hence help establish the professional boundaries of this relationship. Contracts are also usually made with the client and relevant organisations for duty of care and client welfare. Viewed as a role-induction mechanism for the supervisee (Watkins and Scaturo, 2013), the supervision contract can also be useful as a 'statement of agreement' for supervision (Bernard and Goodyear, 2009: 205). Process contracts are suggested by Gilbert and Evans (2000) to enhance the supervisory relationship. A preference of mine is the 'learning contract', advocated by Orlans and Edwards (2001), to promote transparency and collaborative enquiry in supervision. Building on that perspective, my preferred term is that of a 'learning agreement' which is negotiated between the supervisor and the supervisee for the purposes of supervisee learning in the context of providing the best service to clients. It is akin to Leddick's (1994: 1) understanding of supervision when he proposed that 'clinical supervision is the construction of individualized learning plans for supervisees working with clients.'

Learning agreements have a relatively long tradition of use in education and professional training and have been employed at undergraduate and postgraduate levels across a range of disciplines: for example, nursing (Richardson, 1987), social work (Bogo and Vayda, 1998) and medicine (Mårtenson and Schwab, 1993). They have been advocated in the literature as a means to facilitate self-directed learning, encourage ownership of learning and promote commitment to lifelong learning (Brewer et al., 2007; Jones-Boggs Rye, 2008). They have also been adopted in the pedagogical context of work-based learning programmes to facilitate the needs of the relevant organisation, educational institution and the learner (Nikolou-Walker and Garnett, 2004).

With reference to supervision, a learning agreement is a means by which informed consent is gained from the supervisee (Thomas, 2007). In other words, the supervisee is explicitly agreeing to enter into a working relationship with a supervisor who is making clear the terms and conditions, so to speak, of that working alliance. Clarity of role and purpose may provide structures of containment and reassurance whereby the supervisee can feel more secure in the relationship (Gilbert and Evans, 2000; Page and Wosket, 2001). Contracts can be used as a tool for collaborative goal-setting (Hewson, 1999).

Contracts or learning agreements may be seen as reciprocal. While the supervisee is entering into this agreement, the supervisor is also agreeing to provide for and meet certain conditions. This is well articulated by Munson (2002: 43) who views contracts as a 'Bill of Rights' for the supervisee. According to Munson (2002: 43), a supervisee is entitled to a supervisor who provides the following:

1. Regular and consistent supervision.
2. Growth-orientated supervision that respects personal privacy.
3. Supervision that is technically sound and theoretically grounded.
4. Evaluation on criteria that are made clear in advance and based on actual observation of performance.
5. Possession of adequate skill in clinical practice and training in supervision.

What to Expect in a Learning Agreement

Contracting is conducted and implemented in different ways. Some supervisors and supervisees dislike the structure and formality of a written contract and its legalistic connotations (Gibbs, 2009). Some prefer verbal agreements. The difficulty with the latter is that there is no record of agreement to refer to for review or discussion. The first session with a supervisor may also be an anxious meeting; there is much information to process and one can forget the details of agreements. Should difficulties arise, there is no concrete touchstone to which either the supervisee or supervisor can refer back. I recommend a written contract or learning agreement signed and dated by both the supervisor and supervisee with both retaining a copy. This would then form part of the record keeping that is required in supervision.

Again, written contracts can vary from one-page outlines to a detailed information pack. In the US context, many contracts contain a 'professional disclosure statement' made by the supervisor. This details the qualifications and experience of the supervisor and general information about what the supervisee will experience in supervision.

According to Munson (2002), a contract should make explicit the time and frequency of supervision sessions, how learning will be organised (e.g., role-play, audio-visual presentations), how supervision will be provided (individual, group and so on) and the requirements of the agency (e.g., policies and procedures) in which the work will be conducted. Any special conditions of the work will also be detailed and discussed.

A more extensive contract outline is provided by Osborn and Davis (1996: 121) where they recommend that the following areas are discussed and clarified:

- Purpose, goals and objectives of supervision.
- Context of supervision.
- Method of evaluation.
- Duties and responsibilities of supervisor and supervisee.
- Procedural considerations (e.g., how differences will be managed).
- Supervisor's scope of practice.

Similarly, Howard (1997) recommends that the supervisor provides a 'professional disclosure statement' which clearly outlines their qualifications, experience and approach to supervision. He further suggests that clarity is provided with reference to how confidentiality is to be protected and the limits to confidentiality and best practices regarding documentation and record keeping. Boundaries regarding dual relationships need to be explicated, along with strategies for problem and conflict management. Professional indemnity of the supervisee and supervisor also need clarification.

In addition, I include discussion of how and when the learning agreement will be reviewed, how the supervisor may be contacted in the case of an emergency and contingencies in that regard. Details of fee arrangements, if relevant, also need to be explicit. The supervisee may also wish to add their preferences and areas for discussion to the learning agreement. While it provides structure to help negotiate the content and process of supervision, the learning agreement also needs to be held flexibly and reviewed frequently as the supervisee gains experience and competence.

Contracts with Organisations

As with learning agreements between supervisor and supervisee, roles, rights and responsibilities also need to be made explicit when working with an organisation and communicated to all the relevant stakeholders. In the training context, the training course usually provides for these. However, it is important that the supervisee is aware of the content of such contracts. Typically, these will include information on the expectations of each party and performance expectations, including feedback and evaluation.

In summary, a learning agreement can be seen as a supervisory intervention to make explicit the practicalities of the supervision arrangement and help establish professional boundaries. It can further explicate the learning needs of the supervisee in the context of their work and the relevant policies and procedures that facilitate client welfare. Furthermore, the expectations of both the supervisor and supervisee can be explored in this context and any concerns can be aired. A learning agreement can be seen as a 'container' in itself for the supervisory process, providing a 'road map' to navigate the supervisory experience and a framework for integrating learning (Creaner Glen and Creaner, 2010). An example of a basic learning agreement contract pro forma is provided in Appendix 1, which may be expanded or developed as required. For a more extended version, see Sutter and colleagues (2002).

A learning agreement is not a wand that will magically resolve issues or conflicts if they arise. It is, however, a statement of supervision intent and an attempt to articulate the boundaries of a professional relationship. As the supervision process develops, the learning agreement will need to be reviewed from time to time.

REFLECTIVE QUESTIONS

1. What is the purpose of establishing boundaries in supervision?
2. What do you think about using a learning agreement in supervision?
3. How might it help you plan, integrate and evaluate your learning?
4. How might it interfere with your experience of supervision?

8

How to Prepare for a Supervision Session

This chapter has a practical, 'how to' focus, and refers to the process knowledge required of a supervisee. Some strategies are suggested to prepare for and maximise learning in supervision.

Beginning Supervision

One of the themes apparent in practice is that beginning supervisees understandably can be unsure of how best to use supervision in the initial stages, though it is to be hoped that they will receive some role induction from their course and supervisor. Frequently, the learning is in the doing, and in subsequent reflection, and it takes time to settle into the role of supervisee. In the context of group supervision, it also takes time for group members to get to know and trust each other and for the group to establish cohesion (see Chapter 6). With reference to training, it also takes time for a supervisee to identify their learning needs, and it is not unusual *not* to know what one needs to learn. While we do not have empirical confirmation, professional wisdom indicates that as supervisees gain experience and develop professional competence, learning needs will change over the course of their career (Worthington, 2006).

Defining one's personal and professional learning needs takes consideration, reflection and an attitude of openness to continuing professional development. As counsellors and therapists, we are accountable to professional ethics and standards of practice, and it is a requirement to reflect on our professional development in the broader context; hence, there is a greater responsibility to be met beyond our individual learning needs. Supervision is one place where this reflection can be facilitated. There are many analytical tools for assessing one's learning needs (e.g., Belar et al., 2001).

How Does Supervision Work?

While the previous chapters have outlined some of the conceptual thinking and theoretical frameworks that underpin supervision, the actual process and experience of supervision is difficult to capture or articulate. This is due in part to the unique and complex relationship that is supervision and a variety of mediating factors in the persons of the supervisee and supervisor (their worldview, developmental stage, personal and professional experience and so forth), the clients presented and the context of the work. Whether in the role of supervisor or supervisee, no two supervisory relationships are ever the same, in my experience. Supervision is largely experiential and it is in the lived experience that a supervisee gets to know how it works for them. In addition, little guidance currently exists in the literature on how to use supervision effectively (Van Ooijen, 2000: 57). Having said that, there are certain 'givens' in supervision. It is a professional learning relationship, optimally characterised by mutual respect and a collaborative approach to reviewing practice. It is also more than a relationship as there are tasks to be accomplished and goals to be achieved.

Drawing on Power's (2007) framework, the 'boundary of content' (see Chapter 7) refers to what is to be discussed in supervision. In short, anything that relates to the work with clients, and a supervisee's professional development and identity in that regard, are focal supervision content. However, the key focus is always on the client and optimal therapeutic outcomes. Supervision models and frameworks can be a resource for supervisees when thinking through what they need to bring to and get from supervision. As discussed in Chapter 5, supervision models and frameworks can be useful in preparing for and evaluating a supervision session. For example, Proctor's (1987) formative, normative and restorative framework (mentioned in Chapter 1) can help supervisees identify what they want to focus on in a supervision session. The following reflective exercises may be useful in considering how to prepare for and best use supervision at this time.

REFLECTIVE EXERCISES

For each of the exercises answer the questions below

> *Exercise 1*: Take a few moments to reflect on a client with whom you are currently working and by whom you are challenged in some way in your work together and answer the following questions from your theoretical perspective.
> *Exercise 2*: Take a few moments to reflect on a client with whom you are working well and answer the following questions from your theoretical perspective.

Formative learning needs

- In my work with this client, what formative needs do I have?
- What do I think and feel about this client?
- How do I assess and conceptualise their presenting and ongoing difficulties psychologically?
- What theory is guiding the therapeutic relationship and the strategies and interventions I use?
- How effective are my strategies and interventions? How do I know this?

(Continued)

(Continued)

- What are the professional, ethical and legal issues in this case?
- How do I feel about my professional role?
- How does the work help me develop my professional identity?
- What is my development plan: my areas of strength in the work and areas for development?

Normative learning needs

- In my work with this client, what normative needs do I have?
- Is this the best approach with this client?
- What evidence supports this approach with this client?
- What help do I need with case management and record keeping?
- Do I need to liaise with any other professionals?
- What light does my code of ethics shine on these questions?
- Are there any legal considerations?
- What do I need to discuss with my supervisor?

Restorative learning needs

- What support do I need in my work with this client?
- How am I impacted by my client and by our work?
- What self-care needs can I identify here?
- What do I need to implement them?
- How do I feel about presenting this client in supervision?

It may also be useful for the supervisee (and the supervisor) to track the patterns of focus in supervision. For example, if supervisees' learning needs are singularly articulated in terms of case management and normative learning needs, what learning opportunities are being missed regarding restorative and formative learning needs?

While different supervisors have different requirements and styles of supervision, most generally require varying degrees of structure regarding the presentation of client work in supervision. This will also be influenced by the supervisee's theoretical orientation, that of the supervisor and, where relevant, that of the training course. This is something that the supervisee will discuss with their supervisor in the initial learning agreement or contract. While the learning needs of the supervisee are a priority along with client care, how client work is presented may need to be negotiated with the supervisor with reference to the stage of training or qualification. For example, in training, the supervisor may have to meet specific requirements of the training course or accreditation bodies (some stipulate that audio tapes of client work should be presented in supervision for discussion and feedback). See Chapter 12 for further discussion of evaluation.

Supervision methods can vary from supervisor to supervisor and also depending on the therapeutic approach (e.g., art therapy). Some supervisors use role-play frequently, while some may have a preference for verbal presentation. It is hoped that there is flexibility and a range of different strategies employed to facilitate the different learning preferences and needs of supervisees.

Whatever the stage of professional development, getting the best out of supervision requires preparation time before each supervision session. As mentioned, one's theoretical orientation will have implications for how a client presentation is effected. There are many models of case conceptualisation and formulation available pertinent to specific theoretical orientations. In the training context, as a supervisor, I usually tease out with a supervisee the key areas to document, request that supervisees have written up their notes in advance of supervision and provide an overview of the client work as the primary focus of the session. For trainees, requirements are that, insofar as possible, all therapy sessions are audio-recorded (with the written informed consent of the client). It can be an anxiety-provoking and potentially exposing experience to present in such a way and this will need to be teased out with the supervisee in terms of how they implement this with a client and how they feel about doing so. Of course, depending on the client's presenting difficulties, it may not always be possible or advisable to do so. If a particular client is being presented in supervision, an extract of the session being presented in transcript form and an accompanying audio-recording may be required, with all identifying information having been removed.

Any written or electronic recorded client material is considered a record and subject to informed consent and confidentiality. All documents (written or electronic) need to be stored securely and destroyed securely, unless they need to be kept in perpetuity (for example, in mandatory reporting cases). Please see Chapter 9 for ethical and legal implications.

Presenting in Supervision

Supervisee Self-report

One of the most frequent means of presenting in supervision, though from a supervisor perspective probably the least reliable method of providing supervision, particularly for trainees, is that of supervisee self-report. In this format, the supervisee selects what they want to report about a particular client and, consequently, it may be subject to personal bias (Noelle, 2002). While such self-report is optimally guided by the supervisor's questions and reflection, no direct observation is available. Hence, pertinent information may be missed with respect to the therapeutic process.

The Use of Case Notes and Session Transcripts

The content of case notes which are kept after each client session may be the focus of the supervision session. The anonymity and confidentiality of the client needs to be protected in all record keeping and informed consent needs to be secured.

The use of session transcripts allows for some observation of the skills and strategies employed by the supervisee/therapist, albeit it is a limited observation of the therapy session. The use of a transcript presupposes that the session has been recorded (with the client's permission) and has been accurately transcribed by the supervisee. One of the advantages of this method is that it can facilitate supervisee self-reflection on the session prior to supervision and help the supervisee to focus on their specific learning needs in relation to the client. While I consider it a worthwhile endeavour, particularly for trainees and periodically for more advanced supervisees, one of the disadvantages of using transcripts is that it is a time-consuming process to conduct on a regular basis with each client. It can also be experienced as an exposing process for beginners. The secure transportation and storage of transcripts is imperative, and I recommend that they are treated with the same care as case notes and are anonymised and contain no identifying information on the client. From the perspective of the supervisor, the use of transcripts is limited in that nuances of non-verbal behaviour cannot be observed. For example, information regarding tone of voice, eye contact, body language and so forth is not available.

The Use of Video and Audio Recordings

I am an advocate of reviewing in supervision video/audio recordings of client sessions with supervisees to get a first-hand sense of the client and a clear focus on the supervisee's learning needs in relation to their work with the particular client. Of course, this is with the client's (or legal guardian's) prior written permission and informed consent. A video recording allows for direct observation of non-verbal behaviour, whereas an audio recording allows limited access to that.

Reviewing a recorded client session can also be a useful way for a supervisee to self-critique and identify areas of strength and areas for development (Sobell et al., 2008). Used in conjunction with a transcript, it is the nearest one can get to live supervision, and with both the supervisee and supervisor reflecting on the work, it can foster a collaborative approach in supervision.

The use of audio/visual recordings in supervision requires preparation in advance. In addition to gaining written informed consent, I often suggest to supervisees, particularly trainees, to practise the use of recording equipment with a peer prior to implementing this with a client. Reliable equipment is also important. With the rapid advancement of technology in the past decade, there are many choices of equipment available to supervisees. However, it is important to evaluate the appropriateness of the equipment being employed. Recordings are records and as such they need to be treated confidentially, transported safely, stored securely and destroyed in the manner and timeframe agreed with the client, unless subject to statutory regulation (e.g., mandatory reporting).

Time Management

Time management in supervision is always a challenge, particularly if the supervisee has a large caseload or, in the context of group supervision, many supervisees have high case demands. Considering clients' needs and supervisee learning priorities in advance of supervision will help focus in the session. Holding a realistic expectation of what can be achieved in the time available is a joint responsibility between the supervisor and supervisee. However, client emergencies need to be brought to the immediate attention of the supervisor.

REFLECTIVE QUESTIONS

1. How do you feel about bringing a recording of a client session to supervision? What are some of your considerations around this?
2. How appropriate do you think it would be to record a therapy session on your mobile phone? What might be some of the ethical and legal problems and implications associated with that?
3. What consideration do you give to transporting client notes to supervision?

VIGNETTE 1

In the scenario below, the supervisee is a first-year therapy trainee. The supervisee is in their second term of clinical placement in an adult mental health agency and has a caseload of six clients per week.

Supervisor: How are you today?

Supervisee: Good, ya, nothing much going on. I have an assignment due for my course this week and a bit under pressure time wise.

Supervisor: Yes, I well remember the time pressures of training! How is your client work going?

Supervisee: Client work is going fine. A couple of clients didn't show up this week so nothing new since we met last week. I really don't have anything to discuss today, it's all going fine.

Supervisor: Ok – do you want to re-schedule for another time?

With reference to the above scenario, consider the following questions:

- How well do you think the supervisee was prepared for supervision?
- How well do you think the supervisor was prepared for supervision?
- What do you think is going on for the supervisee? The supervisor?
- What ethical/clinical/legal/professional considerations are present here?
- How might the supervisor have balanced challenge with support with this supervisee?
- Do you think the clients have been considered in terms of duty of care?

9

Ethical and Legal Considerations in Supervision

This chapter provides an overview of some of the key ethical considerations in supervision, including informed consent, confidentiality, multiple relationships, disclosure and record keeping as they pertain to the supervisee–supervisor relationship. Equality and inclusive practice is reviewed as it appertains to supervision, and the well-being of the supervisee is considered.

Please note that, while ethical and legal considerations of the therapy context are most pertinent to supervision and will be generally reflected on in this chapter, it is beyond the scope of the chapter to discuss in detail ethical and legal issues as they relate to clients. There are a number of excellent texts available in this regard (e.g., Jenkins, 2007; Bond and Mitchels, 2008; Mitchels and Bond, 2010). The intent here is to provide the supervisee with some areas to reflect upon in the specific context of their relationship with their supervisor, while bearing in mind that all the ethical principles and legal requirements that apply to therapy also apply to supervision.

Developing Ethical Awareness and Sensitivity

Developing ethical awareness and sensitivity is a continuing process and is at the very core of supervision. With reference to ethical maturity, Bond (2013: 10) maintains that, rather than being a destination at which to arrive, 'maturity suggests a quality of engagement in how we respond to the challenges of professional life.' The principles of respect, competence, responsibility and integrity are identified by the British Psychological Society (BPS, 2009) as the pillars of ethical conduct and need to inform all aspects of professional activity for its members.

All of the ethical guidelines and codes of professional practice that apply to counselling and psychotherapy practice also apply to the supervision of that practice. Supervision is also a place where ethical awareness and practice are monitored and modelled by competent supervisors and where supervisees are facilitated and supported to work through ethical dilemmas or legal issues. Furthermore, in relation to ethical and legal awareness, rather than considering that ethical dilemmas or legal implications of client work are isolated events to which the supervisee responds, McGee (2005: 273) contends that 'it is essential to accept ethical and legal issues as potentially omnipresent, and as intimately interwoven with all aspects of clinical and other practice as well as all aspects of training and supervision.' Ethical supervisors, according to Barnett and colleagues (2007: 270), oversee many areas:

> important areas of ethical practice attended to in supervision and modeled appropriately in the supervisory relationship include assessing the supervisee's training needs from the outset and tailoring the training experience to them ... reaching an agreement on the nature and course of the supervisory process and relationship at the outset, providing timely feedback with meaningful recommendations for improvement, maintaining appropriate boundaries, not engaging in exploitative or harmful multiple relationships with supervisees or others, appropriately maintaining clients' and supervisees' confidentiality and breaching it appropriately when required to do so, practicing (and supervising) within one's areas of competence, attending to personal wellness and factors that may impact one's effectiveness and paying appropriate attention to diversity issues.

Barnett et al.'s (2007) profile of an ethical supervisor describes well the relationship, tasks and functions of ethical supervision. Ultimately, and across developmental stages, supervisors monitor the service that is provided to clients, facilitate and promote best practice principles and supervisee compliance therein and evaluate or certify supervisees for training institutions or professional associations (ACES, 1993). Supervisors are also 'accountable for interventions and clinical decisions implemented by their supervisees' (Falvey and Cohen, 2003: 63). The standards of ethical supervision behaviours that the supervisee should reasonably expect that a supervisor will provide have been outlined by Tannenbaum and Berman (1990: 70) as the following:

- Provide supervision only within their areas of expertise and competence.
- Work from a specific model of supervision.
- Maintain ethical boundaries and avoid dual relationships.
- Provide clear and regular feedback and evaluation of the supervisee's competence.
- Be available for supervision.
- Implement a clear supervision contract.
- Be mindful of the financial implications of supervision.
- Maintain professional indemnity insurance.
- Supervise honestly and with integrity.

Informed Consent in Supervision

In the interest of informed consent, the client, who also contracts with the trainee/agency to attend for therapy, is fully informed of the supervisee's status and their supervision arrangements. As previously mentioned, should the supervisee need to audio/video record therapy sessions for supervision and/or educational purposes in training (e.g., written or electronically recorded material for case studies, process reports and so on), permission in the form of written consent needs to be sought and acquired from the client (or legal guardian) prior to the use of their material. The client needs to provide informed consent with reference to how any material that relates to them is stored and subsequently destroyed.

Informed consent is also required for the supervisee to contract for supervision (Thomas, 2007). As discussed in Chapter 7, developing a learning agreement or contract is a means of making the roles, responsibilities and rights of the supervisee and supervisor relationship more explicit. However, rather than a technical exercise, obtaining informed consent in the therapy or supervision context is a process that requires full disclosure of the potential risks as well as benefits, including those associated with engaging in supervision (Thomas, 2010), and the limits of confidentiality in the case of statutory obligations (e.g., risk, child protection).

Confidentiality in Supervision

Another cornerstone of psychological therapy practice, confidentiality is a legal concept, while also being the basis of trust in a relationship that respects the privacy rights of the individual (Bond and Mitchels, 2008). Within supervision, client confidentiality is also protected within the statutory limits regarding risk (for further discussion on legal issues in counselling and psychotherapy, see Jenkins, 2007; Mitchels and Bond, 2010). The limits of confidentiality also apply to the supervisor and supervisee in this instance. Beyond risk, there may be other limits to confidentiality: for example, when reports on the professional development of the supervisee need to be provided to courses or accreditation bodies or in the case of unethical behaviour by the supervisee or issues of fitness to practise. The limits of confidentiality for supervisees also need explicit discussion. In the event of any necessary breach of that confidentiality, due process and informed consent need to be earnestly reflected upon and implemented.

Aligned to the normative function of supervision, the monitoring task of supervision provides for ethical best practice and 'quality control' (Carroll, 1996: 64) and, in the UK (to date), 'supervisors owe a duty of care to clients in an ethical and professional sense' (Jenkins, 2007: 90). Jenkins (2007: 90) distinguishes this from the direct legal liability of the supervisor, which is the case in some US states, and suggests that 'it seems unlikely that supervisors in the UK carry this kind of liability for the work of supervisees.' Mitchels and Bond (2010) also agree that the supervisor holds an ethical responsibility to the supervisee's clients in terms of overseeing competent practice. They also acknowledge that, while causality may be hard to determine legally, 'a supervisor could potentially be held liable … in respect [of a client] of whom the supervisor has provided bad advice and guidance which was then acted upon to the detriment of the client' (Mitchels and Bond, 2010: 40). In terms of confidentiality and monitoring professional ethics, unfortunately there may be times when a supervisor may need to breach supervisee confidentiality in the best interest of the client or, indeed, the supervisee or in the public interest. Again, due process and informed consent are key factors. The hope is that monitoring will become a collaborative task with the supervisee, rather than an act or an experience of surveillance.

Multiple and Dual Roles in Supervision

As discussed in Chapter 7, defining the boundaries of supervision is an important aspect of establishing a professional supervisory relationship. A dual or multiple relationship refers to having other relationships outside the professional therapy or supervision realm (e.g., friend, business or romantic partnerships) which could compromise the integrity of the professional role. Related to the concept of professional boundaries, multiple and dual roles have been a complex area of discussion in therapy, although less attention has been paid to this area in supervision.

Distinctions are made between 'boundary crossing' (which may or may not have a negative impact on the client or supervisee) and 'boundary violations'; the latter are considered as potentially harmful and unethical, particularly with reference to the power differential inherent in helping relationships (Falender and Shafranske, 2012a: 174). Hence, ethical injunctions are placed on such relationships (e.g., sexual, exploitative) between a supervisee and their clients or between a supervisor and a supervisee.

While there are clear ethical guidelines prohibiting dual role and sexual relationships with clients and supervisees, it is still considered one of the more problematic boundaries to manage (Martin et al., 2011). In a professional relationship where empathic engagement with another is a goal, there may be a variety of challenges in the background: for example, where the practitioner is experiencing personal relationship difficulties, where unresolved intimacy issues may impact upon the practitioner and where inexperience in the professional role can blur boundaries. Human sexuality is ever present in relationships, and sexual attraction and feelings may be evoked for a myriad of reasons, particularly if there are already existing vulnerabilities. Consequently, practitioner awareness is key to recognising such potential vulnerabilities and managing this boundary. In contrast to the psychoanalytic perspective of the 'erotic transference' conceptualisation of sexual attraction, Koenig and Spano (2004) propose a human sexuality model for addressing sexual dynamics in supervision and offer the following principles as guidelines for supervisors:

1. Competence in one's knowledge, attitudes, and values about sexuality precedes effectiveness in managing sexual dynamics in supervision;

2. Effective clinical skills are central to integrating sexuality into practice (e.g., confrontation, self-reflection, empathy, exploration of taboo subjects, and normalizing behavior);

3. Supervisors are responsible for initiating discussions about sexuality and focusing them on professional relationships. (Koenig and Spano, 2004: 14–15)

Some dual roles are clearer than others. In training, for example, a supervisor and supervisee may be in many different roles (tutor/tutee; supervisor/supervisee; research supervisor/research student) and each role will need to be clearly defined and con-tracted. As with all ethical matters, the supervisor has the responsibility of monitoring professional boundaries with reference to the supervisee and their client and also with reference to the supervisory relationship. Furthermore, supervisors need to be mindful of the potential of developing a dual role with a client of their supervisee. Discussing potential dual relationships at the outset of supervision and throughout, as required, can help define the parameters of the supervisory relationship and prevent confusion regarding professional boundaries. Consultation with a supervisor or peer can also help clarify these issues.

VIGNETTE 1

You are a final-year student on a counselling training course and have been working with your supervisor for just under a year. As part of your studies, you have developed a workshop on complex trauma. Your supervisor is aware of this as you have consulted with him on a number of occasions as he is an established expert in the area. Your supervisor is very impressed with the outcome of your work and suggests that you and he co-present the workshop at a training day in the agency in which he works.

- What are your initial thoughts/feelings/reactions?
- What do you need to consider?
- Would you agree to co-present? Why/why not?

VIGNETTE 2

You are an experienced practitioner and are ending an 18-month professional relation-ship with your supervisor as they are re-locating to another part of the country. In the final session, your supervisor invites you out to dinner the following week, as their guest, to acknowledge the work you have done together.

- What are your initial thoughts/feelings/reactions?
- What do you need to consider?
- Would you accept the invitation? Why/why not?

Supervisee Disclosure in Supervision

A good supervisory relationship fosters trust and transparency, while being explicit about the monitoring of best practice and evaluation. Getting the best out of super-vision requires the supervisee to be open to the supervision learning process and to disclose to the supervisor areas of concern regarding their clinical practice. Little is known about non-disclosure among experienced practitioners. However, in the training context, research indicates that supervisees can withhold essential information from their supervisor for a variety of reasons and are less likely to disclose issues regarding their dissatisfaction with the supervisory relationship (Hess et al., 2008; Sweeney and Creaner, forthcoming). According to Mehr and colleagues (2010: 103), 84.3 per cent of trainees withhold information from supervisors. The most common non-disclosures relate to their experience of supervision or personal reactions to their supervisors, with other non-disclosures regarding clinical errors, competency concerns and sexual attraction. The quality of the supervisory alliance was related to the level of disclosure.

Worthington and colleagues (2002) suggest that deliberate non-disclosure of information relevant to therapy practice and supervisory responsibilities may be regarded as an ethical issue. In the US context, it may also have legal implications in terms of supervisor vicarious liability to clients.

REFLECTIVE QUESTIONS

1. What issues do you not bring to supervision?
2. Why do you think this is the case?
3. What would facilitate you to bring these issues to supervision?
4. How do you/might you communicate your learning needs to your supervisor?
5. What implications does the non-disclosure hold for your client? For you? For your supervisor?

Equality and Inclusive Practice in Supervision

Psychotherapy and counselling are value-laden practices. As practitioners, our personal frames of reference influence how we view and interact with the world, and as practitioners we bring these worldviews to practice (Remley and Herlihy, 2009). Becoming aware of our biases, assumptions and pre-understandings is a central task in training and a continuing task in professional development. Such self-awareness is fostered by many means and methods; for example, through interpersonal relationships, life events, training and personal therapy. Our assumptions can also be challenged by research (Cooper, 2010) and in supervision as it relates to the practice of supervision and the practice of therapy.

Recent developments regarding multicultural competence in counselling and therapy are becoming more apparent in the supervision literature, highlighting the need for this area to be further developed (Adams, 2009; Falender et al., 2013). With reference to the social interaction dimension of supervision and power-related dynamics, a number of studies has explored this topic broadly in relation to multicultural issues (e.g., Dressel et al., 2007; Ancis and Marshall, 2010) and, more specifically, in relation to gender (e.g., Holloway and Wolleat, 1994; Walker et al., 2007), sexual orientation (e.g., Harbin et al., 2008; Burkard et al., 2009), and spirituality and religion (e.g., Aten and

Couden-Hernandes, 2004; Gilliam and Armstrong, 2012). When multicultural issues are adequately addressed in supervision, it has been shown to enhance the supervisory relationship and increase satisfaction with supervision (Gatmon et al., 2001). Conversely, when such issues are inadequately addressed or the supervisor demonstrates a lack of cultural or supervisory competence, this can negatively impact on the supervisee's emotional safety and confidence (Wong et al., 2013).

Documentation and Record Keeping in Supervision

Documentation and record keeping of client work is an ethical and clinical responsibility for practitioners and a practice that holds legal implications. A record is basically any medium (paper, electronic, audiovisual) that can record and store information (post-it-notes, memos, mobile phones, DVD, computers and so on). Record keeping in supervision serves a number of functions, as it does in therapy, and is governed by the same ethical, legal and professional principles (e.g., Data Protection Act 1998, Freedom of Information Act 2000, court order).

A supervision session record provides a record of what was discussed in the supervision session and records any actions required or taken (see Appendix 2). Again, both record keeping in supervision and record keeping in therapy practice should be discussed with the supervisor during the initial contracting stage, including what record keeping (e.g., record of supervision session, any placement/agency documentation, training/accrediation reports, storage and so forth) will be required as an aspect of informed consent. When in the role of supervisor with trainees, we also discuss countersigning any referral letters/professional reports/mandatory reporting documents in third-party communications.

I recommend that a written record be kept of each supervision session by both the supervisee and supervisor to provide continuity of learning. This, from my perspective, serves to model best practice and the standards of the profession by the supervisor. The supervision session record, at a minimum, should include:

- The date, time and duration of the supervision session.
- The pseudonyms of those attending the supervision session.
- A record of the issues raised and discussed.
- Any case management actions required regarding risk.
- The agreed date of the next supervision session.

When keeping any professional record, it is wise to be mindful of what to record, and assume, though this may not be the case, that the supervisor/supervisee/client or relevant parties will read records. The following questions are useful to reflect upon when keeping a record:

- What needs to be recorded?
- Is it as objective as possible?
- Is it relevant to supervision?

- Would the supervisee/supervisor/client recognise themselves?
- Are there any surprises for them?
- How do I securely store these records?
- How long do they need to be kept?

Technology in Supervision and Ethical Considerations

I have noticed, as a supervisor, that questions relating to technological advances have become more commonplace in supervision in recent years. Frequently, these questions are with reference to ethical considerations in social media use and are certainly challenging traditional boundaries of therapy and bring another dimension to supervision. I have been supervising since the mid-1990s, just as the Internet was becoming widely accessible, when questions regarding contact outside therapy were mainly about the advantages and disadvantages of providing one's home landline telephone number to a client or how to manage accidently meeting a client in a social context. These questions have since evolved to consider the ethical, clinical and potentially legal implications of receiving or sending text messages or emails to clients, using web-based video conferencing for therapy (e.g., Skype), using search engines (e.g., Google) to discover information about clients, and maintaining an online social media presence (e.g., LinkedIn, Facebook, Twitter).

Professional codes of ethics apply to all practitioner activity for those who are members of a professional organisation. However, when considering the use of technology, particularly social media, a number of additional factors and ethical implications need to be taken into account. As suggested by McAdams and Wyatt (2010: 191), 'at present, capabilities for applying technology in counseling and supervision clearly exceed understanding of its implications and, thus, the ability of counselors to ensure that its impact on consumers will be positive.' To that end, professional organisations are responding to the unique challenges presented in this context and have provided additional guidelines for their members. As mentioned, the BACP provide *Guidelines for Online Counselling and Psychotherapy* which also includes a section on online supervision (Anthony and Goss, 2009). The BACP recognises online practice as a specialist area that requires specific training and supervision. With reference to the use of social media, the British Psychological Society (BPS, 2012) provides additional ethical guidelines for members engaging in social media. A further resource is available from Stretch and colleagues (2012) who provide an ethical framework online for the use of technology in supervision.

Supervisee Well-being and Self-care as an Ethical Consideration

As proposed by Carroll and colleagues (1999: 135), self-care includes 'intrapersonal work, interpersonal support, professional development and support, and physical/recreational activities'. Many factors can impact on one's well-being, and in recent years practitioner well-being has received much attention in the literature in terms of the positive and negative impact of training and working in the area of counselling and psychotherapy (Harrison and Westwood, 2009). All practitioners who provide emotional support are susceptible to burnout, vicarious trauma, secondary traumatic stress and compassion fatigue. These are highlighted as risk factors for practitioners who do not attend to their own self-care needs, particularly those who work in trauma contexts (Richards et al., 2010; Rasmussen, 2012).

Professionally, there is also increasing emphasis on the need for helping profession-als to actively seek support and engage in meaningful self-care as an 'ethical imperative' (Norcross and Guy, 2007: 5) and this is also reflected in professional codes of ethics. With its emphasis on reflective practice, engaging in good supervision is cited as one method of enhancing self-care, resourcing oneself and staying dynamic in the work (Howard, 2008; Hawkins and Shohet, 2012). Supervision encompasses a restorative function (Proctor, 1987) to safeguard against the stresses of the work. Practitioners are encouraged to engage actively in 'protective practices' for well-being in the profession (Harrison and Westwood, 2009).

Based on empirical research and experience, and taking into account internal and external contributing factors to practitioner well-being, Norcross and Guy (2007) offer 12 strategies for consideration which I find very useful as a reflective practice tool for supervisees. Interestingly, the authors focus on developing an attitude of self-care in that they concentrate on strategies rather than on specific tasks or behaviours. In doing so, they also acknowledge that individuals have unique self-care needs.

Norcross and Guy (2007) begin by recommending that self-care starts with the per-sonal awareness of the practitioner. Continuing reflection on one's motivations, strengths, resources, needs and vulnerabilities is recommended. The authors encourage consider-ation of the rewards of the work and the satisfaction and privilege inherent as a resource for the practitioner. Awareness of the stresses and 'hazards' of the work allows the prac-titioner realistically to consider what resources are needed to provide scaffolding and support (Norcross and Guy, with Laidig, 2007: 35). Physical self-care is noted as an area of neglect by many practitioners, and the authors suggest that 'sleep, bodily rest, nutrition, exercise and human contact … embody our energy and sense of engagement' (Norcross and Guy, 2007: 64). Developing enhancing relationships, both personal and professional, while maintaining boundaries, again both personal and professional, can be sustaining for helping professionals. Reframing how we think about our work and ourselves in that context can help develop more realistic expectations of ourselves and others, including our clients (Norcross and Guy, with Turkson, 2007: 114). 'Healthy escapes' from work are encouraged to help maintain a good work–life balance (Norcross and Guy, with Karg 2007: 131). The work environment is discussed in terms of managing the demands of the work, considering the physical and organisational environment and optimising the supports available. Internal resources are the focus of the final three strategies, with con-tinuing personal development, meaning-making and creativity-seeking endorsed for the well-being of the therapist.

In summary, Norcross and Guy's (2007) 12 strategies comprise the following catego-ries (see Norcross and Guy, 2007, wherein a chapter is devoted to the discussion of each strategy):

1. Valuing the person of the psychotherapist.
2. Refocusing on the rewards.
3. Recognising the hazards.
4. Minding the body.
5. Nurturing relationships.
6. Setting boundaries.
7. Restructuring cognitions.
8. Sustaining healthy escapes.
9. Creating a flourishing environment.
10. Undergoing personal therapy.
11. Cultivating spirituality and mission.
12. Fostering creativity and growth.

Based on these areas, I suggest some reflective practice questions below:

- *Valuing the person of the psychotherapist*

  - What was your initial motivation to train as a therapist?
  - What is your continuing motivation?
  - What are your strengths in the work?
  - What are key areas for development?
  - What comprises your support system?

- *Refocusing on the rewards*

  - What do you most enjoy about your work?
  - What satisfaction do you gain in your work?
  - How does your work benefit your life?

- *Recognising the hazards*

  - How familiar are you with the literature on the stresses experienced by helping professionals?
  - What do you find most challenging in your work?
  - What presenting issues/client groups are most challenging for you to work with?
  - Who can offer support?
  - What resources can you draw upon?

- *Minding the body*

  - How do you take care of your physical self?
  - How is your sleep, nutrition, exercise routine?
  - What resources do you draw upon?

- *Nurturing relationships*

  - How supportive is your work environment?
  - What would enhance your professional relationships?
  - What would enhance your personal relationships?
  - What supportive relationships would help you?

- *Setting boundaries*

  o How well do you keep boundaries between yourself and others?
  o How well do you maintain boundaries between your personal life and your professional life?
  o How do you transition from your work life to your personal life?
  o How adept are you at saying 'no'?

- *Restructuring cognitions*

  o What negative self-talk do you engage in about your work?
  o About yourself? What would help you re-frame this?
  o How well do you extend empathy to yourself?

- *Sustaining healthy escapes*

  o What healthy escape behaviours do you engage in?
  o What helps you 'get away from the office'?
  o How do you know when you need a break?
  o What healthy escapes would you recommend to a colleague?

- *Creating a flourishing environment*

  o How do you think your organisational context impacts on your work?
  o How do you think your work environment impacts on your work?
  o How do you make your work environment your own?

- *Undergoing personal therapy*

  o How do you take care of your psychological self?
  o When would you seek personal therapy?
  o What self-development activity is restorative for you?

- *Cultivating spirituality and mission*

  o What nurtures you in your work?
  o How does your work contribute to meaning in your life?
  o What keeps you inspired in your work?

- *Fostering creativity and growth*

  o How do you keep enthusiastic in your work?
  o What variety is available to you in your work?
  o What would you like to do next in your career?
  o What will support you to achieve your career goals?

REFLECTIVE EXERCISE

You have contracted with your individual supervisor to meet for a total of 25 sessions of 60 minutes duration per session. This has also been contracted with your training institution and clinical placement, and this is a requirement of your course's accreditation criteria. It is your first experience of supervision. However, the agency in which your supervisor works is very short staffed, and in the past three supervision sessions your supervisor arrived 10 minutes late and had to leave early – these sessions averaged 30 minutes. As your client caseload is increasing, you are becoming anxious that you are not getting what you need from supervision or meeting the hours required. To date you have not discussed this with anyone as you do not want to rock the boat and also feel empathic to your supervisor and the organisational demands made on her time.

- What are the issues in this?
- What resources might you draw upon?
- How might you proceed?

10

Good and Not So Good Supervision

This chapter will explore effective and ineffective supervision with reference to the key purposes of supervision: primarily, the well-being of the client and the professional development of the supervisee. With these in mind, the chapter will consider some of the impacts and outcomes that supervision has for clients and supervisees. It also considers how supervisee and supervisor contribute to effective or ineffective supervision as reported in the literature.

Supervision Impacts and Outcomes for Clients

The welfare of the client needs to be held as the defining feature of supervision and therapy practice – this is why supervision primarily exists. To revisit Bernard and Goodyear's (2009: 7) definition of supervision as 'the simultaneous purposes of enhancing the professional functioning' of the supervisee, 'monitoring the quality of professional services offered to clients … and serving as a gatekeeper for those who are to enter the particular profession', client welfare and the development of supervisee competence is the dual purpose of supervision. Consequently, to ascertain the effectiveness of supervision, both therapy outcomes for the client and competence development for the practitioner need to be considered (Falender et al., 2013). In both cases, the evidence on the effectiveness of supervision is scarce (Wheeler, 2003; Falender et al., 2013).

Similarly, according to Ellis and Ladany (1997: 485), the 'acid test' of good supervision is whether or not it positively impacts on client outcome. In his review of 20 years of research on the impact of clinical supervision on client outcome (1981–1997, none existing from 1997 to 2001), Freitas (2002) identified and critiqued ten studies, many of which contained significant methodological errors. Supervision research, particularly in relation to client outcome, was seen as a complicated endeavour. The conclusion reached by Freitas (2002: 266) was that, cumulatively, the studies reviewed were useful to 'guide future exploration in this complicated area of research'. Whether supervision is of value to the client seemed inconclusive from these studies.

In their systematic review of the literature entitled 'The impact of clinical supervision on counsellors and therapists, their practice and their clients', Wheeler and Richards (2007) report on two additional studies and include the study by Steinhelber and colleagues (1984) reviewed by Freitas (2002). These provide some evidence that supervision positively impacts on client outcome (Steinhelber et al., 1984; Milne et al., 2003; Vallance, 2004). However, Wheeler and Richards (2007) state that these were short-term studies and none provided sufficient evidence to confirm a positive impact on client outcomes. A clear gap emerges when, as Holloway (1995: 92) maintains, 'the supervisor's raison d'être is to ensure that the trainee can deliver effective service to the client'. Freitas (2002) explains that supervision research on client outcome is linked to the complex endeavour of determining psychotherapy impact on client outcome; therefore, the two subjects need to develop in tandem to some extent.

From their review of the literature, four research findings have been identified by Bambling and colleagues (2006: 318), which indicate that supervision may contribute to client outcome. They suggest that (a) an effective supervisor relationship enhances the modelling process for supervisees which, in turn, may enhance their therapy skills with their clients; (b) supervision enhances confidence in the practitioner; (c) the development of core counselling skills is enhanced by supervision; and (d) supervision may help the supervisee to manage the therapeutic relationship. Bambling et al. (2006: 318) state that further research is clearly indicated to establish whether or not clients are impacted by their therapist undertaking supervision.

Client protection is frequently cited as a 'gatekeeping' function of supervision (Carroll, 1996; Feltham, 2000; Bernard and Goodyear, 2009), although, as Feltham (2000: 19) cautions, the supervisor can never know with certainty what happens in the therapy dyad. Further research in this area is called for by Feltham (2000). Specifically, he calls for a deliberation on the importance of considering client outcomes and a greater emphasis on the evaluation of supervision. Furthermore, he cautions that, in light of increasing professionalisation demands, the welfare of the client may frequently get lost in the administration of regulations for accreditation.

Impacts and Outcomes for Supervisees

Considering the central role that supervision plays in counselling and psychotherapy training, and subsequently over one's career, establishing what is effective and ineffective in supervision is essential. In that case, what do we know about what supervisees and supervisors find helpful and hindering in supervision in terms of their competence development?

In looking at the gold standard of effective supervision outcomes or, in Norem and colleagues' (2006: 40) terms, 'stellar supervision outcomes', the authors interviewed 12 experienced supervisors about what they considered as successful supervision outcomes (professional development in supervision) from their work with their supervisees and reported what they considered to be the essential key factors. Norem et al. (2006: 40) identified the supervisee attributes given in Table 10.1 as contributing to

Table 10.1 Supervisee attributes contributing to excellent outcomes

Attribute	Definition
1. Maturity	From a variety of life experiences, including exposure to diverse ideas and people, stellar supervisees acquire information and gain understanding of themselves and the counselling profession. Their maturity contributes to the development of autonomy.
2. Autonomy	Supervisees have sufficient self-confidence and self-efficacy to try new behaviours as well as accept and evaluate feedback from others. They take an active role in the counselling and supervision processes.
3. Perspicacity	Supervisees have requisite knowledge, strong theoretical background, and skills for counselling. They demonstrate the ability to use rational processes. They demonstrate characteristics associated with wisdom, including cognitive complexity, empathy, discernment, sagacity, intuition and insight.
4. Motivation	Supervisees are committed to professional growth and excellence in counselling practice. They proactively develop professional skills and knowledge. They exceed minimum requirements.
5. Self-awareness	Supervisees are able to identify their strengths and weaknesses. They actively self-monitor. They are aware of their emotional experiences and responses. They are amenable to exploring their experiences related to clients and supervisors.
6. Open to experience	Supervisees are willing to try new techniques and strategies. They are experienced risk takers. They consider different perspectives. They welcome feedback.

Source: Norem et al. (2006: 40). Reproduced with the kind permission of Texas Counseling Association.

excellent outcomes. It may be daunting for the beginning supervisee to reflect on these attributes, and certainly challenging for the supervisor to consider, as the authors suggest, how these attributes can be facilitated and developed in supervision.

From their systematic review of research, Wheeler and Richards (2007) identified the following studies as indicative of supervision having a positive impact upon supervisees. As discussed and detailed by Wheeler and Richards (2007: 62–3), these included:

- an increase in supervisee self-awareness (Borders, 1990a; Raichelson et al., 1997);
- the development of skills (Borders, 1990a; Worthen and McNeill, 1996; Patton and Kivlighan, 1997; Raichelson et al., 1997; Ogren and Jonsson, 2003);
- an increase in self-efficacy beliefs (Efstation et al., 1990; Ladany et al., 1999; Cashwell and Dooley, 2001; Lehrman-Waterman and Ladany, 2001);
- development in theoretical orientation (Guest and Beutler, 1988; Milne et al., 2003); and
- feeling supported (Strozier et al., 1993).

Timing and frequency of supervision were seen as an influencing factor on the outcome of supervision (Couchon and Bernard, 1984; Steinhelber et al., 1984). While such evidence exists, Wheeler and Richards (2007) note that only two of the 18 studies reviewed could be classified as good-quality research, and most were conducted with trainees in a US context. While supervisees report that supervision is valuable (Wheeler and Richards, 2007), evidence for this remains scarce.

An interesting point for reflection is provided by West (2003: 124) when quoting a conference discussion with Nicholas Ladany in 2002, who stated that 'when supervisees are asked about their experience of supervision: one-third say it is excellent, one-third say it is good enough, one-third reply that it is problematic in some way.' It would be interesting to discover the reasons for the response of each 33 per cent, and how factors to do with the supervisee, the supervisor, the relationship and the context of supervision have contributed to experience of supervision.

What is 'Bad' Supervision?

In considering 'good' or effective supervision, the notion of 'bad' or ineffective supervision is also pertinent in identifying what is good by virtue of its absence. In their paper, which is interestingly entitled 'A profile of lousy supervision', Magnuson and colleagues (2000) report their interviews with 11 experienced counsellors (10 of whom were also experienced supervisors). The aim was to investigate ineffective supervisors' practices. They identified six overarching principles of what they considered 'lousy supervision', summarised in Table 10.2.

Supervisor behaviours that contributed to 'lousy supervision' were identified in a number of spheres (e.g., organisational/administrative; technical/cognitive; and relational/affective). The areas of supervisor deficit identified by Magnuson et al. (2000: 200–1) are shown in Table 10.3. Clearly, these findings support the need for the supervisor to monitor their practice through consultancy and supervision. It further supports the need for adequate training in supervision.

Table 10.2 Overarching principles of 'lousy supervision' according to Magnuson and colleagues (2000)

	Principle	Supervisor behaviour
1.	Unbalanced	Supervisor's inability to focus on all aspects of supervision
2.	Developmentally inappropriate	Supervisor's inability to respond to the changing needs of supervisees
3.	Intolerant of difference	Supervisor's wanting to produce replicas, little room for supervisee's initiative
4.	Poor model of professional/ personal attributes	Poor modelling on the part of the supervisor, boundary violations, lack of confidentiality
5.	Untrained	Supervisor's lack of training, skill and professional maturity
6.	Professionally apathetic	Supervisor's lack of commitment to the client, supervisee or profession

Source: Magnuson et al. (2000: 200). Reproduced with the kind permission of John Wiley and Sons.

Table 10.3 General spheres of 'lousy supervision' according to Magnuson and colleagues (2000)

Organisational/administrative

Fails to clarify expectations

Fails to provide standards for accountability

Fails to assess supervisee needs

Fails to be adequately prepared

Fail to provide purposeful continuity

Fails to provide equitable environment in group supervision

Technical/cognitive

Perceived as an unskilled practitioner

Perceived as an unskilled supervisor

Perceived as an unreliable professional resource

Provides vague and abstract feedback

Focuses primarily on micro-skills and techniques

Relies on a single primary model; unidimensional

Fails to appreciate supervisee's theoretical model or orientation

Relational/affective

Fails to provide a safe environment; intrusive

Gives too much or too little corrective feedback

Gives too much or too little affirming feedback

Shows insensitivity to supervisee's professional and developmental needs

Avoids issues between supervisor and supervisee

Is guided by external criteria

Imposes personal agenda

Source: Magnuson et al. (2000: 200–1). Reproduced with the kind permission of John Wiley and Sons.

While a number of studies have investigated the experiences of the supervisee, few studies exist on the contribution of the supervisee to good or bad supervision from their perspective. A study was conducted by Wilcoxon and colleagues in 2005 and focused on 'Supervisee's contributions to lousy supervision outcomes' from the perspective of supervisors. A qualitative phenomenological enquiry produced four general categories of supervisee contribution to lousy supervision as given in Table 10.4.

The implication of these perceptions of supervisees' contributions certainly raises concerns about supervisee suitability for training and fitness to practise. While both of these studies focus largely on a supervisor perspective, the findings are useful to consider broad areas that may contribute to ineffective supervision. They bring to light the need for a forum whereby supervisees have a right of reply and a safe place to report unethical and ineffective supervision. The need for further research is clearly indicated

Table 10.4 Spheres related to supervisees' contributions to 'lousy supervision' outcomes according to Wilcoxon and colleagues (2005)

Sphere 1 Intrapersonal development	
Limiting factors at entry	Emerging/enduring manifestations
• Psychological limitations • Unresolved issues	• Fearful of change • Unwilling/unable to examine self
Sphere 2 Interpersonal development	
Limiting factors at entry	Emerging/enduring manifestations
• Social limitations • Lack of sensitivity/respect	• Unable to grasp client's perspective • Unwilling/able to accept feedback • Defiant/avoidant in supervision
Sphere 3 Cognitive development	
Limiting factors at entry	Emerging/enduring manifestations
• Limited cognitive and intellectual ability • Lack of cognitive complexity • Limited analytical ability	• Unable to conceptualise • Rigid
Sphere 4 Counsellor development	
Limiting factors at entry	Emerging/enduring manifestations
• Limited skills and limited knowledge base • Limited motivation for learning • Limited understanding of counselling process	• Mechanistic focus • Unwilling to grow and change

Source: Wilcoxon et al. (2005: 39). Reprinted with the kind permission of Texas Counseling Association.

to identify appropriate intervention strategies for supervisors to address the difficulties presented and deal with fitness to practise issues with experienced practitioners as well as with trainees (see Chapter 11).

Regarding the supervision of trainees within the UK and Irish context, the training institutions and the supervisor, who is optimally contracted by these organisations, hold suitability and fitness to practise responsibilities. Ideally, both parties are supported by the institution to address concerns. However, supervisors of experienced practitioners can feel quite isolated in their evaluative and gatekeeping role. While they have the authority and remit from their accrediting bodies to evaluate competence, the process of interrupting or potentially ending the practice of a therapist deemed unfit is arduous and can be fear-provoking, not least of all from a legal perspective.

As the process of supervision occurs in relationship, it is reasonable to assume that both the supervisee and supervisor contribute to good or bad supervision. The organisational contexts that surround the supervisory relationship may also be influential in how supervision is experienced: for example, the nature of the contract, confidentiality, whether or not the supervisor is also a line manager, instances when agency policy conflicts with the ethical principles to which one subscribes and so forth (Carroll, 1996; Copeland, 1998, 2002, 2005). Again, little research has been conducted with regard to the impact of the organisation on the supervisory relationship or process, particularly from the supervisee's perspective (Davy, 2002).

In their mixed method study (n = 126) on negative experiences in supervision, Ramos-Sánchez et al. (2002: 197) reviewed the impact of trainee supervisee developmental level, attachment style and experiences of negative events on the supervisory alliance and satisfaction levels. Their findings from the qualitative analysis indicated that 20 per cent of their participants experienced negative events across four categories: namely, 'interpersonal relationship and style; supervision tasks and responsibilities; conceptualisation and theoretical orientation; ethics, legal and multicultural issues' (Ramos-Sanchez et al., 2002: 200). Negative experiences included a lack of support, personality clashes, conflict regarding the goals of therapy, inadequate feedback, a judgemental approach, supervisor's lack of clinical, ethical, legal and/or multicultural competence. Those who described negative experiences also described poorer supervision relationships. They were less satisfied with supervision and experienced diminished confidence in their competence which they felt negatively impacted upon the supervisee/therapist–client relationship. The conclusion of Ramos-Sánchez et al. (2002: 201) was that 'it can be inferred that development of supervisees is contingent upon a good supervisor, a strong supervisory relationship, and a swift, effective response to negative events that may occur in supervision.'

Harmful Supervision

The quality of supervision provided can be understood on a continuum from effective to harmful. While the majority of supervisees report positive and effective supervision experiences, there is an increasing body of literature emerging that has investigated ineffective and harmful dimensions of supervision experiences, particularly with trainees (e.g., Magnuson et al., 2000; Ellis, 2001: 8; Gray et al., 2001).

Ellis (2010: 108) distinguishes between 'inadequate' and 'harmful' supervision as experienced by the supervisee when he proposes that 'inadequate' (bad) supervision may occur when the supervisor is 'unable or unwilling to enhance the professional functioning of the supervisee, monitor the quality of the professional services offered to the supervisee's clients, or serve as a gatekeeper to the profession'. While the supervisee does not necessarily experience direct harm in this instance, inadequate or neglectful supervision may have a negative impact on the client. Ineffective and potentially harmful supervision is supervision that does not take into account the learning needs of the supervisee and the treatment needs of the client. It also fails to monitor client progress, treatment outcomes and client well-being, and hence may be understood as potentially harmful to the client.

Harmful supervision as experienced by the supervisee, according to Ellis (2010: 108), refers to 'supervisory practices that result in psychological, emotional, and/or physical harm or trauma to the supervisee' whether through direct action on the part of the supervisor or a supervisor not acting in a professional manner with the supervisee.

What Facilitates 'Good' Supervision?

From the literature reviewed and from my professional experience, it is clear that good supervision needs to happen collaboratively and in a relationship that is characterised by mutual respect, encouragement, psychological safety, openness to addressing conflict, challenge and transparency regarding the functions and tasks of supervision. The question 'what facilitates good supervision?' is directly related to the question I have frequently asked as an educator – 'what facilitates learning?'

Rogers and Freiberg's (1993) concept of 'freedom to learn' has been most influential on my thinking about learning. The facilitative conditions of empathy, congruence and unconditional positive regard, and a seeking to be in psychological contact with the other, are necessary in all learning relationships. These concepts, together with a systems awareness of the personal, professional, ethical, legal and social context in which learning occurs, and an openness to learning from many sources, are the foundation concepts of all learning relationships, as I perceive them.

Supervision is about facilitating learning. In their 2005 survey, Lizzio and colleagues investigated supervisees' perceptions of the learning processes and outcomes in their supervision relationships. Participants of this study were psychology graduates ($n = 264$) working towards registration, who were asked about their perceptions of the manner in which their supervisor facilitated learning, how they as supervisees approached supervision and what they considered to be the outcomes of effective supervision. Findings confirmed that the supervisory relationship was conceptualised as a learning relationship. Findings also indicated that supervisees constructed the supervisor's approach to learning as 'didactic' or 'facilitative'. A facilitative approach resulted in more positive evaluations of supervisor ability and a decrease in supervisee anxiety. Supervisees also valued supervisor flexibility regarding these approaches to learning. A facilitative approach was also positively correlated with the effective outcomes.

The optimal learning environment is well summarised by Hutt and colleagues (1983: 120) when they suggest that 'the interpersonal climate facilitates growth and learning. "Mistakes" can be made without "failure"; and behavior, attitudes, and feelings can be explored without questioning the worth of the individual.' There is, in Rogers and Freiberg's (1993) words, 'freedom to learn'. One of the recurring concerns I hear from beginning supervisees are fears that they may be personally judged as not good enough. Psychological safety is also a recurring theme for beginning as well as experienced supervisees (Weaks, 2002; Carter et al., 2009).

In considering good supervision experiences for supervisees, two variables in particular (although there are many) seem to recur in the literature: namely, power differentials in the supervision relationship and supervisee anxiety.

Power Dynamics in Supervision

Supervision can be experienced at times as paradoxical: supervisees are encouraged to be open, with appropriate disclosure, and to bring clinical challenges and mistakes to supervision, while, at the same time, they realise that this is an evaluative professional relationship and one's competence may be evaluated as lacking based on what is brought for review.

References to the power differential in the hierarchy of supervision are frequently made throughout this text. The power dynamic is also frequently referred to in the literature as an intrinsic feature of the supervisory relationship (e.g., Green and Dekkers, 2010; Hernández and McDowell, 2010; Copeland et al., 2011). While many definitions and philosophical explications of power in relationships exist (for example, Weber, Foucault and others), there are many perspectives and contextual variables associated with power in the larger social, political and economic systems.

Many of the challenges in supervision emanate from the hierarchical nature of the supervisory relationship, the power differential inherent therein and individual reactions and responses, from both the supervisee and supervisor, to that given. Notwithstanding that there are frequently differences in training, qualification and expertise between supervisor and supervisee, from my perspective it is how that power is effected that is the issue. Supervisors always hold a gatekeeping function and monitor normative standards. While this also needs to be balanced by incorporating the restorative and formative functions, gatekeeping is ever present.

Drawing on game theory and the work of Eric Berne (1964), Kadushin (1968), with reference to supervision in social work, suggested that when there is a perceived power disparity in a relationship, people may consciously or unconsciously initiate various psychological 'games' or manipulative behaviours to feel more powerful. According to Berne (1964: 44), such psychological games involve 'a recurring set of transactions, often repetitious, superficially rational with a concealed motivation'. The goal of the exercise is to win the game: hence, protecting against anxiety and preserving self-esteem, which is considered as the pay-off. Kadushin (1968), and later Hawthorne (1975), suggested that both supervisees and supervisors can play psychological games in supervision as a method of mediating stress.

With reference to supervisors, Hawthorne (1975) proposed that, depending on their own dynamics, some but not all supervisors – those who felt uncomfortable with the authority inherent in the role and less experienced as a supervisor – were most likely to initiate psychological games to avoid assuming appropriate authority. Two particular avoidance of authority strategies or games were identified by Hawthorne (1975: 179): namely, 'games of abdication' and 'games of power'. In the former, the supervisor can abdicate responsibility to a third party (e.g., the agency or organisation) in a manner that still preserves the illusion of authority, helpfulness, effectiveness and so forth, but does not meet the needs of the supervisee. While agency demands can be a legitimate challenge to supervisors in this context, Hawthorne suggests that it is problematic when these games are played for manipulative and coercive purposes. Some examples of such abdication games include (Hawthorne: 1975: 180):

'They won't let me': In this game, the supervisor expresses willingness to help but projects responsibility onto another party (e.g., the organisation) for the decision-making required without exploring alternatives. For instance, a trainee/supervisee asks their supervisor if it

is possible to attend a forthcoming workshop in the agency as it would be a useful resource for their client work. The supervisor says that they admire the supervisee's initiative, totally supports the idea but considers that it is a waste of time to ask the agency manager as they are unlikely to permit a trainee to attend a staff workshop.

'*Poor me*': Here, the supervisor inappropriately elicits sympathy from the supervisee for not meeting supervision requirements. As an example, the supervisor frequently cancels or curtails supervision sessions and suggests that they would not do so, only they are inundated with paperwork/the agency is demanding an urgent report/they have an emergency meeting and so on.

In the 'games of power' strategy, the supervisor assumes all power, fosters dependency in the supervisee and, again, in doing so relinquishes the authority of the supervisory role. For example (Hawthorne, 1975: 182):

'*Remember who's boss*': this is an authoritarian stance where power and control are exerted upon the supervisee to develop passivity and not allow negotiation or discussion. There are frequent reminders to the supervisee that evaluation is impending.

'*I'm only trying to help you*' or '*I know you can't do this without me*': This game again seeks to engender dependency and passivity in the supervisee, this time based on the knowledge and experience of the supervisor. The supervisor here assumes incompetence on the part of the supervisee, although this is presented in the guise of helping.

In psychological game playing, it takes two parties to play the game. However, as supervision is a hierarchical relationship, the supervisee may not feel sufficiently confident or empowered to challenge this behaviour. On the other hand, abdicating responsibility to the supervisor may also meet a need in the supervisee.

Psychological games may also be played by some supervisees. These relate to establishing equity in power, mediating the demands made by the supervisor and controlling the supervisory relationship (Kadushin, 1968). It is interesting that these games are often referred to as 'resistance' in supervisees, but not so in similar supervisor behaviour. Some of the strategies employed by supervisees, according to Kadushin (1968: 25–6), include psychological games that serve to lessen the demands made on the supervisee by the supervisor. While these strategies where provided in the context of social work, they may also be relevant to cross-disciplinary supervision contexts. For example, the supervisee game 'Be nice to me because I'm nice to you' (Kadushin, 1968: 25) is a game of collusion whereby, for instance, the supervisee might sycophantically state that 'You are the best supervisor I ever had', thus seeking to diminish potential challenges by the supervisor. Another example is the game 'Evaluation is not for friends' (Kadushin, 1968: 26). In this case, the supervisee seeks to establish a social relationship rather than a professional relationship with the supervisor, thus seeking to mitigate potential negative evaluation.

According to Liddle (1986), the primary objective of resistant behaviour is self-protection. Resistance is not always problematic: it may well be employed as a protective strategy in the face of some real threat whether it be to one's self-esteem, sense of confidence or competence.

Anxiety in Supervision

Anxiety is a frequently reported emotional reaction to supervision, particularly for beginning therapists (Mehr et al., 2010; Mastoras and Andrews, 2011) and has been attributed to a number of domains, including a lack of understanding of what happens in supervision (Berger and Buchholz, 1993), attachment patterns of the supervisee (Renfro-Michel and Sheperis, 2009), power differentials (Nelson et al., 2008), feeling inadequate in the role of therapist (Worthen and McNeill, 1996) and as a symptom of vicarious trauma (Adams and Riggs, 2008). Evaluation anxiety is also noted as it pertains to competence and performance review (Lizzio et al., 2005). While not confined to supervision, evaluation anxiety may be understood as a natural human reaction to feared negative outcomes, such as discomfiture, humiliation or rejection (Donaldson et al., 2002: 261). Interestingly, while anxiety is anticipated in the supervisory process, Ellis (2010) surmises that its omnipresence is questionable and may be more related to feelings of competence than intrinsic to the experience of supervision.

However, a certain level of anxiety is normative and an appropriate response to new learning situations. It takes time to develop competence and confidence in the role of therapist. Nevertheless, high levels of anxiety may impede the learning process. From my experience with new supervisees, some anxiety relates to not knowing what supervision entails and knowledge of this is, of course, not the exclusive responsibility of the supervisee. Role induction to supervision has been identified as a means to reduce anxiety (Ellis, 2010). Bahrick and colleagues (1991: 437) discovered that role induction elicited positive changes for beginning trainees relating to clearer conceptualisations of supervision and clarity about how best to use supervision.

It makes sense that the more the context, relevant roles, rights and responsibilities of both the supervisee and supervisor are explicated, the more the supervisee will know what is expected of them. On the other hand, new supervisees have also related to me over the years that, while role induction was important, relevant and necessary, it was only the real-life experiencing of the supervision process for themselves that rendered clarity.

In working with an experienced practitioner, anxiety may arise from knowing precisely how supervision has worked in the past, particularly if there have been negative supervision experiences. Furthermore, concerns and anxiety about one's competence as a practitioner may be a feature of continuing therapist development across the career lifespan (Thériault and Gazzola, 2005). Consequently, this may provide a raison d'être for career-long supervision.

REFLECTIVE QUESTIONS

1. As you reflect on your therapy practice, how do you think that supervision affects therapy outcomes with your clients?
2. How do you experience power in the supervisory relationship?
3. What support and resources can a supervisee draw upon to manage a poor supervision experience?

Professional Considerations in Supervision

This chapter will focus on issues related to professional practice, including fitness to practise and professional standards in supervision. It provides an example of the accreditation requirements for supervision from the perspective of the British Association for Counselling and Psychotherapy (BACP). It presents some of the current debates regarding the benefits and challenges of professionalisation in the field.

Fitness to Practise

Ethical practice and profession best practice are by necessity dialogical in nature. Ethical practice is professional best practice. When concerns arise about a supervisee's fitness to practise, there are a number of frameworks, including an ethical framework, that may be a resource for both the supervisee and the supervisor.

In the UK, the Health and Care Professions Council (HCPC, 2012a, 2012b; see www.hcpc-uk.org) currently regulates 16 professions, among which are included practitioner psychologists, social workers and art therapists. As an independent regulatory body, its purpose is ultimately to protect the public, and to achieve this end it applies standards for training and registration and implements a fitness to practise process for its registered members. The HCPC (2012b: 2) defines 'Fitness to Practise' as:

> When we say that a professional is 'fit to practise' we mean that they have the skills, knowledge and character to practise their profession safely and effectively. However, fitness to practise is not just about professional performance. It also includes acts by a professional which may affect public protection or confidence in the profession. This may include matters not directly related to professional practice.

While the HCPC encourages the self-regulation of fitness to practise and also to manage these issues locally in the first instance, any member of the public can make a complaint against a registrant. If this occurs, each complaint is investigated by the HCPC and, if found valid, a formal public hearing may be conducted for which a number of outcomes can be returned. The complaint may not be upheld due to a lack of evidence or perhaps the issue may have subsequently been remediated and will therefore be dismissed. Other outcomes include cautions, conditions attached to practice, suspension or being struck-off the register. A registrant may have their name removed from the register if discovered to be a fraudulent or incorrect entry. A registrant may also voluntarily opt to have their name removed from the register. The HCPC publishes annual reports on fitness to practise hearings, and if the final hearing demonstrated that a fitness to practise complaint was upheld, details of the complaint, the outcome of the hearing and the individual's name are published in the report and available on the HCPC website.

The types of complaints generally refer to issues of competence or professional conduct. In the list of complaints made to the HCPC (2012a) in 2011–12, poor record keeping, poor clinical judgement, failure to gain informed consent and breaches of confidentiality are among the fitness to practise issues cited. It is also useful to note that in its investigations of a complaint, the HCPC also takes into account remediation efforts made by the practitioner.

Similarly, to protect public welfare, most professional bodies have a self-regulatory statement on fitness to practise and an accompanying complaints procedure. For example, the BACP's *Ethical Framework for Good Practice in Counselling and Psychotherapy* (2013b: 7/40) states the following with reference to 'Fitness to Practise':

> Practitioners have a responsibility to monitor and maintain their fitness to practise at a level that enables them to provide an effective service. If their effectiveness becomes impaired for any reason, including health or personal circumstances, they should seek the advice of their supervisor, experienced colleagues or line manager and, if necessary, withdraw from practice until their fitness to practise returns. Suitable arrangements should be made for clients who are adversely affected.

The BACP has very clear procedures for 'expressing a grievance or making a complaint' about a BACP member (BACP, 2012: 1). The BACP also encourages the complainant to attempt to resolve the issue with the individual or organisation involved prior to making a formal complaint, though it recognises that this is not always possible. A complaint against a BACP member needs to fall within certain parameters, as outlined by the BACP Professional Conduct Procedure. This will then be reviewed by a Professional Conduct Panel and a Professional Conduct Hearing may ensue. However, while the outcomes of these hearings do not have any legal implications, sanctions may be applied to the BACP member, and in some instances, if the hearing concludes that a serious fitness to practise issue is evidenced, the individual's membership/registration may be revoked. In this instance, an appeal can be made. In addition, the outcome of the complaint, if upheld, may be published on the BACP website or in the association's *Therapy Today* journal.

In their systematic review of BACP misconduct allegations under Article 4.6 between 1998 and 2007, Symons et al. (2011: 262) found that the nature of the complaints brought against BACP members included bringing the BACP and the reputation of the profession into disrepute, misrepresenting membership status and ethical breaches.

While the above information is not intended to be alarming or anxiety provoking, the reality remains that fitness to practise and other professional issues exist in the field. Codes and standards of practice are there for the protection of the public and, in this context, the client. Similarly for the trainee, standards of training are present to evaluate fitness to practise and included within this is the role of supervision; while it serves a formative and restorative function, it also serves a normative function.

It is a fact of life and of professional practice that there are times when a practitioner's effectiveness may be diminished due to a variety of reasons (ill health, life stresses, unresolved psychological issues and so forth). When fitness to practise issues arise for the therapist, supervision may be an invaluable professional support and source of guidance in dealing with and managing such challenges. The supervisor also has a responsibility to monitor fitness to practise issues with all supervisees, irrespective of their developmental level. It can be a most challenging time for both the supervisor and supervisee, if a formal complaint is made against them or if they self-identify an issue. In my experience as a supervisor, I have generally found that the majority of supervisees were highly aware of issues that might impede best practice. However, I am mindful that there also may have been times when issues were perhaps left undisclosed and of which I, as a supervisor, remained unaware.

Fitness to practise is a continuing process. The Health Professions Council (HPC, 2008: 14; subsequently the HCPC), in their research monograph *Continuing Fitness to Practise*, acknowledges the role of supervision in ongoing fitness to practise monitoring:

> Supervision, including peer supervision, mentoring, reflection-on-practice and case review, offers many opportunities for assessment of practice, learning and development by the practitioner or by colleagues and managers. The process results in improved learning, practice delivery and communication and produces evidence to support the HPC's CPD standards and audit.

Professional Requirements for Supervision

Supervision is a requirement by a number of professional bodies (for example, the BACP, UKPC, BPS) across one's career lifespan for counsellors/therapists, supervisors and trainers. The BACP's *Ethical Framework for Good Practice in Counselling and Psychotherapy* (2013b: 7/33) requires the following: 'There is a general obligation for all counsellors, psychotherapists, supervisors and trainers to receive supervision/consultative support independently of any managerial relationships.' With reference to supervised practice of counselling and psychotherapy trainees, the BACP currently requires its accredited training courses to provide 150 hours of supervised practice. The BACP recommends a combination of individual and group supervision and, more specifically, a 1:8 hour ratio of supervision to client work, delivered not less than fortnightly, is required.

In counselling and psychotherapy, while a qualification signals entry into the profession, a period of supervised practice is still required before professional accreditation as a counsellor/therapist is possible. For the purposes of accreditation and post-qualification, the BACP also requires 'an ongoing contract for counselling/psychotherapy supervision for a minimum of 1½ hours per month for each month in which practice is undertaken'.

BACP COUNSELLOR/PSYCHOTHERAPIST ACCREDITATION SCHEME (2013)*

Standard For Accreditation

Eligibility Criteria 1–5

When you apply and throughout the assessment process, you must be:

1. A member of BACP
2. Covered by professional indemnity insurance

When you submit your application you must be

3. Practising counselling or psychotherapy
4. Your training and supervised practice: you must have undertaken training and supervised practice to meet one of the following criteria:

EITHER:

4.1   You have been awarded a qualification from a BACP accredited training course

AND

- Have been in practice at least three years when you apply for accreditation
- Have at least 450 hours of supervised practice accumulated within three to six years (they do not have to be consecutive years)
- Of the 450 hours at least 150 of the hours of supervised practice must be after the successful completion of your BACP accredited course
- Have been supervised for at least 1½ hours per month throughout the period of practice submitted

OR:

4.2   You have successfully completed and received an award for practitioner training that:

- Included at least 450 hours of tutor contact hours
- Was carried out over at least two years (part-time) or one year (full-time)
- Had a supervised placement as an integral part of the training
- Covered theory, skills, professional issues and personal development

---

*Reprinted with the permission of the British Association for Counselling and Psychotherapy

AND

- Have been in practice at least three years when you apply for accreditation
- Have at least 450 hours of supervised practice accumulated within three to six years (they do not have to be consecutive years)
- Of the 450 hours at least 150 hours of supervised practice must be after you have successfully completed your practitioner training
- Have been supervised for at least 1½ hours per month throughout the period of practice submitted.

5. Supervision: you have an ongoing contract for counselling/psychotherapy supervision for a minimum of 1½ hours per month for each month in which practice is undertaken.

Note: Please check the BACP website (www.bacp.co.uk/accreditation) as criteria are frequently updated.

In addition, part of the BACP accreditation criteria requires applicants to submit to various reflective practice exercises which includes a reflection on how supervision influences practice:

CRITERION 9   PRACTICE AND THE USE OF SUPERVISION

9. Practice & Supervision: *in your case material account for … how supervision influences your practice by:*
9.5 Describing the awareness you have gained through reflection in and on supervision
9.6 Showing how you apply that awareness in your practice.

Similar requirements are articulated by the Irish Association for Counselling and Psychotherapy, who hold a reciprocal relationship with the BACP. The British Psychological Society (BPS) also requires formal supervision arrangements in the education of counselling and clinical psychologists and post-training (see BPS, Division of Clinical Psychology, Policy Document on Continued Supervision). What these various criteria suggest is that counsellors and psychotherapists, from the outset of their training, need to be mindful of supervision and to be active agents in their supervision, both in terms of requirements (in training and for accreditation and post-accreditation purposes) and in terms of the impact of supervision on their practice and reflective practice therein. Annual accreditation renewal is required for BACP members who wish to practise.

Professionalisation

There has been quite extensive and appropriate debate in the field on the continuing professionalisation of counselling and psychotherapy, and this continues as evidenced in discussions concerning statutory regulation among the health professions (see Totton, 2010; Murphy, 2011). Arguments against professionalisation, many of which have existed for many years, are varied and range from concerns about developing a 'culture of surveillance' (West, 2003) to more recent concerns about promoting 'defensive practice' (Totton, 2010; Murphy, 2011) and suppressing creativity within the profession (Davies, 2009).

The 'dynamics of the mandatory' (Feltham, 2000: 9), particularly in relation to career-long supervision, has been encompassed within this larger discussion (Grant and Schofield, 2007). As summarised by Wosket (2012), these arguments are based on concerns that there is little evidence to confirm that career-long supervision enhances professional development. Mandated supervision can 'infantilise' experienced practitioners, undermine professional autonomy and ultimately become an 'empty ritual' (Wosket, 2012: 170). Furthermore, supervision may veil bad practice, as much supervision relies largely on third-party accounts. In his article 'The culture of psychotherapy supervision', West (2003) paints a grim scenario when he describes two professionals meeting for a supervision session. The supervisee is present because it is deemed necessary by their profession. The work presented is selective as the supervisee fears a negative response from the supervisor. Where supervision is mandated for the career of the therapist, West (2003) suggests that such a scenario may be a lifelong, fruitless experience.

A further point of contention is raised by Feltham (2000: 9) when he reviewed the implications of 'the dynamics of the mandatory' for supervisees. He proposes that mandated supervision may be considered as a discriminatory practice when the financial costs of supervision are taken into account. In a broader context, LeShan (1996: 91) offers the following unequivocal perspective:

> A therapist who is not in supervision should be regarded either with suspicion or awe. He or she is making a statement that they have learned all that is needed for one of the most complex problems in existence – helping others to be as fully human as possible.

In acknowledgement of some of the problematic questions raised above, Wosket (2012) encourages critical reflection and the engagement of supervisors in such debates in a spirit of openness. As supervision holds accountability to, and responsibility for, client welfare – a goal which also underpins the professionalisation of counselling and psychotherapy – there is common ground and a potential shared goal.

REFLECTIVE QUESTIONS

1. As a supervisee, what are your thoughts on fitness to practise issues?
2. What do you consider the purposes of professionalisation?
3. What do you consider to be the advantages and disadvantages of professionalisation?
4. How does professionalisation of therapy and supervision influence your client work?

VIGNETTE

You are part of a weekly supervision group with five other group supervisees. The group has been working together for three weeks and you are just getting to know each other. One of the group members sent you a 'friend request' on her social media network, which you accepted. When you visit this person's webpage, you notice that she has been writing about her experience in group supervision. She writes that she is really enjoying the supervision experience. She also writes that she is feeling heard and supported by the group members but not by the group supervisor about whom she writes some derogatory comments.

- What are your initial thoughts on this scenario?
- How might you respond to this?
- Would you discuss it with other group members? Why/why not?
- Would you discuss it with the group supervisor? Why/why not?
- What informs your decision-making on this?
- What resources are available to you in this regard?

12

Feedback and Evaluation in Supervision

Giving and receiving feedback are discussed from the perspective of the supervisee and supervisor and as a strategy to facilitate learning. The evaluation task in supervision is also presented, and key issues regarding this task are considered.

Giving and Receiving Feedback

Feedback can be a powerful learning intervention. Verbal feedback concerns the sharing of thoughts and feelings in relation to a particular phenomenon. There is frequently an assumption that feedback means negative or corrective feedback and this is also apparent with regard to evaluation. Feedback can relate to any dimension of supervision, but does need to be relevant to the supervisee's developmental level and learning goals. It can be about the supervisee's professional development and progress, about the client's progress, and/or the supervisees' strengths as well as areas for development. Feedback needs to be balanced. It can be resourcing and supportive and, ideally, a two-way process with one's supervisor. Consider the scenario whereby the supervisor and supervisee are in a supervision session, the supervisee presents their client work and the supervisor makes no observation on anything the supervisee did or did not do. The supervisee, in turn, makes no comment on the lack of verbal feedback. I expect non-verbal feedback would become obvious in a short space of time. I also expect it would be a brief session.

Feedback seems to be taken on board more readily when there is a low risk to self-esteem, but this is also mediated by the quality of the feedback, how and when it is provided and may produce either positive or negative consequences (Hattie and Timperley, 2007). It involves content (what is being said) and process (how it is being said and how it is being heard). Nicol (2010: 507), with reference to written feedback in education which is relevant to supervision, states that feedback is 'not a monologue' and, to be effective, it needs to be dialogical in nature. Feedback ideally is the conversation that happens between the supervisor and supervisee. It will, of course, be influenced by the supervisor's and supervisee's perception of what constitutes good therapy and good practice and the context in which supervision is conducted.

Whether it is individual, group, peer or team supervision, giving and receiving feedback are necessary skills. They are also necessary skills in therapy. Experience is not sufficient for learning to occur. While much is written, particularly in the education domain, about the necessity of feedback and how to deliver it most effectively, the actual experience of giving and receiving feedback may be different (Nicol and Macfarlane-Dick, 2006). Some useful reflective questions are posed by Carroll and Gilbert (2011: 107) when they ask: 'when someone says to you "I want to give you some feedback", what do think? What do you feel? What do you do?' Whether the feedback in question refers to strengths or areas for development, giving and receiving feedback can be emotionally impactful and challenging to accommodate. In training, supervisees are in a constant feedback loop from tutors, peers, supervisors, clients and themselves. However, it is also important for supervisees to develop balanced self-evaluation strategies and identify their areas of strength and areas for development. In other words, in order to develop self-efficacy and begin to trust their clinical judgement, supervisees need to be able to self-evaluate.

Supervisee Perspectives on Feedback

In her study on 'Trainee preferences for feedback and evaluation in clinical supervision', Heckman-Stone (2004: 28) identified the following trainee preferences for feedback and evaluation, namely: 'balanced feedback (positive and negative), accurate feedback based on direct observation, immediate and frequent feedback, a collaborative relationship in which goals and feedback are mutually agreed upon, a positive relationship … openness, clear and specific feedback, and suggestions for improvement'. Among the factors highlighted, the prevalent issues identified by trainees related to receiving balanced feedback which also highlighted strengths, and frequent feedback which allowed for a collaborative discussion.

Feedback and evaluation are not the same thing. However, feedback is the means and method by which assessment and evaluation are communicated. In supervision, feedback is an essential mechanism of learning, and regular feedback ought to be provided in each supervision session. Several models of feedback are available, but generally all recommend that supervisor feedback is given in a timely manner, relates to specific learning outcomes, is both supportive and challenging, focuses on strengths as well as areas for development, builds on previous feedback, and is motivational and respectful of the supervisee as a learner.

Supervisor Perspectives on Feedback

Different supervisors have different styles of giving feedback. While the intention in supervision is to work towards an equal relationship, there is always a power differential presented by the task of monitoring and the gatekeeping function of supervision. Clarity regarding the evaluation and assessment criteria needs to be made explicit in the initial contract and revisited periodically as the supervisory relationship develops

Some supervisors may feel that corrective feedback will negatively impact upon a supervisee's self-esteem. However, Green (2011: 87) argues that 'supervisor's over concern about student self-esteem can lead to avoidance of negative feedback or giving feedback that is too vague to be useful.' An interesting study was conducted by Hoffman and colleagues (2005) in which they asked 15 supervisors to provide three examples of times when they had provided feedback to supervisees; in this instance, the supervisees were trainees. Specifically, they were asked about one example in each of the following categories: one example of feedback that was easily given, one where it was difficult to give feedback, and one where feedback was withheld. Feedback that was easy to communicate related to clinical issues. In contrast, feedback that was difficult to relate concerned clinical, professional or personal issues, and feedback that was withheld related to personal or professional issues. In the latter categories, the supervisee's lack of openness was implicated. Supervisors highlighted the negative impacts of withholding feedback and subsequently regretting having done so. Hoffman et al. (2005: 6) identified factors that facilitated feedback: namely, when the supervisee was open to feedback; when the supervisor had expertise in the area; when there was a strong supervisory relationship; when timing for feedback was good; when there was a clear need for feedback; and when outside support related to giving feedback was available.

SUPERVISEE SELF-FEEDBACK EXERCISE

Reflect on your client work over the past week and consider the following questions:

- What aspects of your work have you noticed have improved over the past few weeks?
- What was the best intervention you made with your client this week?
- How do you know this?
- How do you feel when you think about your client work?
- How do you think of yourself as a therapist/counsellor?
- What areas over the past week would you like to develop further?
- What resources can you draw upon to help you achieve this?

What is Evaluation in Supervision?

'Professional evaluation is defined as the systematic determination of the quality or value of something' (Scriven, 1991). This definition presupposes that the quality and value have been established and that criteria exist whereby these criteria can be measured. In recent years, there have been developments in establishing evidence-based core curricula for practitioner training in therapy (e.g., the British Association for Behavioural and Cognitive Psychotherapies, Core Curriculum Reference Document).

Gould and Bradley describe the task of evaluation as 'the conundrum of supervision' and, in the absence of a clear definition of evaluation in this context, offer the following pertinent questions for consideration:

1. What are the criteria to be evaluated?

2. Who is evaluated and who evaluates?

3. Where and when does evaluation take place?

4. How is evaluation conducted in supervision?

5. Why is evaluation problematic? (2001: 271–2)

Evaluation in supervision is viewed by Bernard and Goodyear (2009: 20) as the 'nucleus' and 'defining aspect of supervision'. Evaluation is also the task that clearly distinguishes supervision from therapy (Inskipp and Proctor, 1995), although it is important to bear in mind that evaluation is one supervision task among many.

What is Being Evaluated?

In the first instance and throughout supervision, the key area for evaluation is client outcomes. The continual question for the supervisee and supervisor is whether or not therapy is helpful, useful and effective for the client. This is a key focus of each supervision session for counselling and therapy practitioners. It is also essential that supervision is experienced as useful to the supervisee in terms of their professional development.

In terms of other criteria to be evaluated, Gould and Bradley (2001) suggest that such criteria have been largely derived from professional standards and accreditation criteria. Bernard and Goodyear (2009: 20) also refer to the assumption in the field that 'criteria chosen or derived from professional standards reflect competent practice' with little outcome evidence to support this assumption. Various initiatives (e.g., Department of Health, 2008) and attempts are being made to define areas of competence in both supervision and therapy (see Roth and Pilling, 2009; Falender et al., 2013).

In the absence of supporting evidence, Bernard and Goodyear (2009: 21) offer some guidelines for addressing the difficulty, and, first of all, suggest that the supervisor needs to distinguish between 'formative' and 'summative' evaluation. The supervisee also needs to be aware of these distinctions. Both the terms 'formative' and 'summative' were coined by Scriven (1967) in the field of education with reference to the methodology of evaluation. 'Formative' in this context refers to evaluation that is given when there is time to address the issues or deficits raised. It concerns itself with 'progress and process rather than outcome' (Bernard and Goodyear, 2009: 21) and is delivered in feedback throughout the process of supervision with the intention of enhancing the developmental direction of the supervisee. On the other hand, 'summative' evaluation concerns itself with interim or final outcome. It is an overall evaluation that predefined goals have been achieved in full. In a training context, this usually occurs formally during and/or at the end of the placement contract.

To distinguish between formative and summative evaluation, an interesting analogy is offered by Stake (2004: 170), 'when the chef tastes the soup, it's formative evaluation, and when the guests taste the soup, it's summative evaluation.' Bernard and Goodyear (2009) suggest that most of the supervisory engagement concerns itself with formative evaluation and that summative evaluation may also be demanding of the supervisor.

In considering the areas of evaluation for supervisees at all developmental stages, the broad domains of counsellor education within a competence framework refer to requisite knowledge, skills, attitudes and values, the ability to integrate and apply these in practice and to reflect upon and evaluate the outcomes in practice (see Roth and Pilling, 2009). Supervision concerns itself with all these domains in the context of applying psychotherapy theory to best practice. While the notion of competence is relevant and valuable, it is challenging for therapy training to operationalise some of the core values on which it is predicated within a competence framework. For example, in a profession that prizes the person of the therapist, their authenticity in the therapeutic process, their self and other awareness in that regard, it is difficult to measure these qualities objectively as a competence. A key point for supervisees is that there is clarity regarding the evaluation and assessment criteria which needs to be made explicit in the initial contract and revisited periodically as the supervisory relationship develops.

The 'When and Where' of Evaluation

The 'when and where' of evaluation refers to the location of the evaluation and the timing and frequency of evaluation. In training, the location is often within the training institute or placement agency and the timing and frequency are pre-determined. As in all supervision sessions, privacy and uninterrupted space are required. Evaluation is not a corridor conversation; rather, a collaborative reflection on the work to date. Ideally, the supervisee will have self-evaluated with reference to the evaluation criteria and this should be part of the collaborative review.

Supervisees should know well in advance when evaluation will take place and with whom this will be conducted. For example, some training courses may conduct an end of placement review which involves the discussion of a collaboratively written summative evaluation, and a course tutor may be present with the supervisor for the evaluation discussion. Other courses require the placement supervisor to conduct a collaborative written evaluation with the supervisee and submit it to the course for review. There may be a follow-up discussion with the supervisee and a course director or representative. Different courses have various methods of conducting summative evaluation. The key point for supervisees is that they should know well in advance how, when and where they will be evaluated and have collaborative involvement in the process. Ideally, this will have been discussed and detailed in the initial contract or learning agreement along with the criteria for evaluation.

As mentioned, the supervisory contract or learning agreement is an essential component of good supervision. It is vital that both supervisee and supervisor know where they stand in relation to their respective roles, responsibilities and rights in the context of a learning relationship. These form part of the 'how' of evaluation as raised by Gould and Bradley (2001). They suggest that evaluation is an exercise of power that highlights the power differential in the supervisory relationship. While the intention in supervision is to work towards an equal relationship, there is always a power differential presented by the tasks of monitoring, evaluation and the gatekeeping function of supervision. Although supervision is not synonymous with evaluation (Borders, 1990b), the consequences of poorly conducted evaluations within a poor supervisory relationship are described as 'long-lasting and devastating to both the supervisee's personal and professional life' (Gould and Bradley, 2001: 278).

As previously mentioned, the supervisory relationship is the container in which all supervision tasks, including evaluation, are conducted. With reference to creating a learning environment conducive to evaluation, Bernard and Goodyear recommend that the following ten conditions be present:

1. Supervisors must remember that supervision is an unequal relationship

2. Supervisors need to state clearly their administrative as well as clinical roles

3. Supervisee defensiveness should be addressed openly

4. Individual differences should be addressed openly

5. Evaluation should be a mutual process and a continuous process

6. Evaluation must occur within a strong administrative structure

7. Premature evaluations of supervisees should be avoided

8. Supervisees need to witness the professional development of their supervisors

9. Supervisors must always keep an eye to the relationship, which influences all aspects of supervision

10. No one who does not enjoy supervising should supervise. (2009: 25–7)

Post-training, practitioners applying for accreditation as a counsellor or therapist generally (though this may vary among the professional associations) need to provide a supervisor's report in addition to other evidence in support of the application. For example, those currently seeking accreditation for the first time with the BACP (2013a) are required to submit an assessment from a contracted supervisor in support of the application, along with other documentation (see Chapter 7 for further requirements). In addition to questions regarding the practicalities of the supervision contract (frequency, length of time and so on), the supervisor will be asked to provide information on the supervisee's applied theoretical orientation, their understanding of the BACP *Ethical Framework for Good Practice in Counselling and Psychotherapy* (2013b) and how this awareness is demonstrated in practice. Supervisors are asked to comment on how the supervisee uses supervision and on their case material in general. Supervisors are asked to detail what action would be taken if the supervisee was working outside their competence and/or demonstrating poor standards of practice.

For more experienced practitioners seeking re-accreditation, the process seems less intensive in terms of supervisor evaluation as no report needs to be submitted, though the BACP reserves the right to contact a supervisor. Furthermore, the BACP randomly selects a portion of applications for auditing, and in this case a confirmatory statement is required from the supervisor.

Evaluation as a Reciprocal Process

The question 'who is evaluated and who evaluates?' is an interesting one posed by Gould and Bradley (2001), and they acknowledge that the supervisee is the primary recipient and the supervisor is the evaluator. Nonetheless, they encourage reciprocity within the evaluation process and the use of evaluation instruments in supervision. Evaluation tools have been compiled by the following authors: Bernard and Goodyear (2009: 326); the Supervisory Styles Inventory (Friedlander and Ward, 1984); the Group Supervision Scale (Arcinue, 2009); the Evaluation Process within Supervision Inventory (Lehrman-Waterman and Ladany, 2001); and the Supervisory Working Alliance Inventory for Supervisor and Supervisee (Efstation et al., 1990). However, as many of these were developed in trainee contexts, they may not be relevant to experienced practitioners.

One instrument that I find most useful across the supervision career span is the Helpful Aspects of Supervision (HAS) for Supervisors and Supervisees, adapted in 1993 from Llewelyn's Helpful Aspects of Therapy (HAT) form (Llewelyn, 1988; see Appendix 10). Both the supervisor and supervisee form comprise the same seven questions, and the forms are completed shortly after a supervision session. The supervisee is asked to discuss a helpful event or events that occurred in supervision which was significant to them and/or their client work. They are also asked to rate the helpfulness of the event. In addition, supervisees are asked to discuss any unhelpful event(s) they experienced in the session. Similarly, the supervisor is asked to identify any helpful or unhelpful event that occurred in supervision for the supervisee. Discussing the outcomes of the session evaluation presents an opportunity for the supervisee and supervisor to share their perspectives. When used routinely, it offers information on the pattern of supervision in terms of what is experienced as helpful and unhelpful by the supervisee. It is also a means by which the supervisor can review the session and provides an opportunity to address any difficulties that are arising. The HAS is also a useful practice-based supervision research tool (Wheeler et al., 2011).

In defining supervision as a learning relationship, evaluation is explicit in that definition: learning objectives and outcomes need to be evaluated for a learning cycle to be completed. If the function of supervision is to monitor and provide a gatekeeping stance on client welfare and facilitate supervisee professional development (Holloway, 1995), then supervision, by its very nature, 'must be evaluative' (Watkins, 1997: 4). Evaluation is not, however, the end point in supervision: it is rather a part of the learning process.

Supervision and the Challenge of Evaluation

For the supervisee, evaluation can raise concerns about psychological safety, about being judged, particularly judged unfairly, and may evoke feelings of shame. No less than therapy – and while every effort can be made to work towards equality in relationship – there is an inherent power differential in supervision, compounded by its evaluative nature, throughout the career lifespan of the supervisee. It may be interesting for supervisees to know that supervisors also find the task of evaluation most challenging. As Bernard and Goodyear (2009: 20) contend, 'most supervisors are troubled by evaluation' and see it 'as a necessary evil'. They propose that, as many supervisors were first trained as psychotherapists, there is a tendency towards a facilitative rather than an evaluative role, and there may be a professional identity conflict. It was also a finding in my own research (Creaner, 2008) where participants felt very ambivalent about evaluation and also felt anxious about the profound responsibility it entailed. For example, I recall one participant saying 'I don't like it. It seems almost to contradict what you're saying about the job. I've never actually been able to work that out in my head but it has to be done.'

REFLECTIVE QUESTIONS FOR SUPERVISEE PERSPECTIVE

1. Why evaluate in supervision?
2. What do you consider the main areas for evaluation?
3. How do you feel about being evaluated?
4. How might you empower yourself in the evaluative process?
5. How do you want evaluation to be delivered?

VIGNETTES

- *Beginning supervisee*: You are in the second term of a three-year therapy training course and attend supervision weekly with a supervisor external to the course. You feel anxious about your client work and that you will never know enough, but find supervision very useful in this regard. You are unsure of where you stand developmentally with your peers. While you like your supervisor and feel you learn a lot in supervision, you feel dissatisfied with the amount of feedback you are receiving. Your supervisor reviews your recorded sessions regularly with you and is encouraging of you as a trainee. They tell you that they will alert you if there are any difficulties, but you wonder if they are being 'too nice'.

    o What are some of the possible issues here for the supervisee? For the supervisor?
    o How might these be addressed appropriately in supervision?

    (Continued)

(Continued)

- *Experienced practitioner:* You are an experienced counsellor and have been accredited for ten years. You have an active private practice and see approximately 15 clients per week. You value supervision and attend individual supervision on a weekly basis. After a three-year productive supervisory relationship with a supervisor who has now retired, you have recently contracted with a newly registered/accredited supervisor, who has a different theoretical orientation from yours, and have met for three supervision sessions. At the end of supervision, you feel 'interrogated' and wonder about the level of corrective feedback your supervisor is providing. You are beginning to feel somewhat 'de-skilled' despite your experience.

  o What are some of the possible issues here for the supervisee? For the supervisor?
  o How might these be addressed appropriately in supervision?
  o What resources can you draw on to address these issues?

13

Endings in the Learning Relationship and the Opportunities Ahead

This chapter will reflect on a much-neglected area in the literature, namely the ending of a supervisory relationship and contract. It will also outline continuing professional development with reference to supervision training. Supervision competencies and key areas for consideration in supervision training curricula are also discussed.

Endings and Beginnings in Supervision

Endings are part of the human condition and intricately linked to the basic human connection: in psychoanalytic terms, the attachment bond between parent and child (Bowlby, 1969). Endings also call to the fore existential reflections about the meaning of experience as one reviews the past. It may also be a time to look forward to new beginnings and, generally, ending with one supervisor signals thoughts of beginning with a new supervisor.

The ending or termination of supervision has received little attention in the literature. However, there are some inferences that may be made from the termination literature available in therapy, though this also is limited (Creaner, 2011b). Ending in therapy can be understood as an intrinsic part of the therapeutic process and, optimally, a consequence of the client realising their goal; in Schlesinger's (2005: xi) words, 'ending is what psychotherapy is all about.' In contrast to the prevailing ideas that termination primarily evokes experiences of loss, Quintana (1993: 426), with reference to short-term therapy, proposed a movement from the 'termination as loss' metaphor to a 'termination as transformation' metaphor which is pertinent for supervision endings.

As in therapy, supervision is generally a time-limited professional relationship. In some instances, supervisory relationships may extend over many years, though in training they tend to be shorter term and usually parallel the duration of clinical placement requirements. Ending a supervisory relationship may evoke a number of feelings and responses from both supervisor and supervisee, depending on the quality of the supervision relationship, the nature of the ending and prior experiences of endings. Endings also present an opportunity to review the work done and explore future possibilities in career direction. Supervision is also the context wherein supervisees process their endings with clients. In training, ending the supervisory relationship may be occurring in parallel with the trainee experiencing multiple endings with clients at the end of a placement contract. Managing multiple and simultaneous endings may be arduous for trainees and have considerable impact on them (Creaner, 2011b) and this is clearly an area for supervisory containment (Power, 2012). In addition, how the supervisory ending is managed may also provide modelling for the supervisee for their endings with clients.

As discussed in Chapter 2, the attachment style of the supervisor and supervisee provides a useful conceptualisation of the supervision relationship (Pistole and Watkins, 2005; Foster et al., 2007; Pistole and Fitch, 2008) and the separation that occurs in endings. A qualitative study conducted by Cooney (2010) explored endings in individual supervision as experienced by trainees. This phenomenological enquiry explored the experience of eight participants in relation to their experience of ending their individual supervisory relationship while they were in training. The key findings revealed that the ending highlighted the overall supervisory experience and was 'a microcosm of the entire supervisory relationship'. A secure attachment in the supervisory relationship facilitated the supervisee to be open, take appropriate risks and develop professionally. It also facilitated them to reconcile any differences, celebrate their work together and prepare to separate and move forward towards collegial relationships and independence. The experience of a secure base was well illustrated by one participant who said: 'So it was almost like a secure base I could go off and do my stuff and come back and reflect on how it worked out ... The supervisor here represented a very confident parent.'

The ending to a supervisory relationship may be initiated by the supervisee or supervisor for many reasons. The reasons will obviously influence how the ending is perceived and experienced. Endings can be the result of a supervisee or supervisor moving location, deciding that this supervision relationship is not a good match or deciding to end for financial reasons. It may also be the consequence of retirement, illness, fitness to practise issues and so forth.

At all developmental levels, preparation for ending a supervisory relationship begins with the initial contract when the duration of supervision is discussed. While formative feedback is usually provided throughout the relationship, the ending may generally signal a summative assessment and evaluation. Ideally, there will also be time for the supervisee to provide feedback to the supervisor. As discussed, evaluation should present no surprises as the supervisee ought to be aware of the relevant criteria from the outset, and continuing formative feedback should have signalled any areas requiring development and issues arising ought to have been flagged in advance of the final evaluation. While frequently being a formal evaluative time, a good ending provides an opportunity to look back, to review and celebrate the work done and to look forward to further consolidating learning in professional practice, to engaging in a new supervisory relationship and to planning for future career development.

Continuing Professional Development: Supervision Training

Often described as the 'next step' in continuing professional development, many experienced supervisees are interested in training to be a supervisor. In recent years, a number of training courses have developed and range from online training to professional training or undertaking a formal qualification in supervision (see Appendix 5 for a sample of training programmes currently available). With developing standards in practice, experience in the role of psychotherapist and supervisee is deemed necessary but no longer sufficient training for becoming a supervisor. The area of supervisor training has developed exponentially in the past few years partly because of the growing awareness that the role of supervisor is distinct from that of therapist/counsellor. The growing importance and the essential nature of supervision are reflected in acknowledgement of the need for formal training in clinical supervision by psychologists, psychotherapists and mental health and health care professionals (e.g., McMahon and Errity, 2013).

Many professional associations (e.g., the British Association for Counselling and Psychotherapy [BACP], the British Association for Behavioural and Cognitive Psychotherapies [BABCP]) have developed accreditation criteria for supervision, and all psychotherapy associations either require or recommend that their supervisors have varying degrees of professional development, which may or may not include a requirement for dedicated training in supervision.

Currently (2013), the British Association for Counselling and Psychotherapy has two separate accreditation schemes for supervisors: accreditation as a supervisor of individuals and accreditation as a supervisor of groups. Accreditation as a supervisor bestows 'senior accredited status' (BACP, 2013c). For accreditation as a supervisor of individual counsellors and therapists, in addition to being an accredited BACP member holding professional indemnity insurance, the following eligibility criteria apply:

- Be in practice as a counsellor/psychotherapist supervised at a minimum of 1.5 hours each month.
- Have undertaken a minimum of 150 hours of supervised counsellor/psychotherapist practice post-accreditation.
- Be in practice as a supervisor of individual counsellor/psychotherapist(s).
- Have undertaken at least 90 contact hours of supervision with counsellors/psychotherapists over a minimum of two years.
- Have in place arrangement(s) for access to consultative support for the supervision work.
- Be able to show professional development activity(ies) to support counselling/psychotherapy and/or supervisory work within the previous 12 months.*

Note: Please check the BACP website as criteria are frequently updated (see BACP, 2013c).

---

*Reprinted with the permission of the British Association for Counselling and Psychotherapy

Similar criteria apply for group supervisor accreditation. It seems that the apprenticeship model is advocated here as no specific training qualification in supervision is listed as a requirement.

With supervision competencies, training curricula and standards largely undefined, systematic enquiry into the complexities of supervision training is essential if supervision is to develop congruently within the profession (Proctor, 1994).The complexity of the issues raised in the preceding chapters supports the need for the training of supervisors, a position that has been advocated by many others in the literature (Holloway and Carroll, 1996; Watkins, 1998; Scott et al., 2000; Falender et al., 2004; Falender and Shafranske, 2007; Hawkins and Shohet, 2012).

Competence in Supervision

The principle of practising within one's competence appears in most of the codes of ethics and practice of which I am aware. It is also a bias of mine and I concur that training is a necessary requirement to provide competently for the learning needs of supervisees, to transition from the role of psychotherapist to supervisor and to provide optimally for client welfare. With increasing demands for accountability and clinical governance, I suggest that it is, at the very least, unwise for the practitioner's personal and professional well-being to engage in an intervention for which they are inadequately prepared.

The work of Stoltenberg (2005: 858) offers a broad definition of competencies: he states that 'competencies consist of relevant knowledge, skills, and attitudes that affect practice, and they are developed and enhanced by professional training.' With reference to developing teacher's professional knowledge, Goodson (2003: 7) claims that 'the joining of "stories of action" to "theories of context" is especially imperative. Without this kind of knowledge, teaching becomes the technical delivery of other people's purposes.' It strikes me as relevant for both the trainer and the supervisor as the dynamics of relationship process and context are integral to the practice, education and training of supervisors and the educative function of supervision.

Competencies become swiftly outmoded and require continual updating, as cautioned by Argyris and Schön (1974: 143): 'professional skills of yesterday and today will not be adequate in the future.' With advances in teaching and learning technology, methods of learning are constantly expanding. The provision of supervision by means of the Internet and video conferencing is currently being developed and offered to practitioners and will need to be reflected upon in the context of supervision training.

In their paper 'Defining competencies in psychology supervision', Falender and colleagues (2004) make a concerted call for supervision training standards and competencies to be established. Acknowledging that supervision is a domain of professional practice, but that standards and requirements for formal training have been ignored, they present a comprehensive competency framework which encompasses knowledge, skills and attitudes/values. In addition, cognisance is taken of developmental factors, ethical and legal issues, 'social contextual factors and issues of education and training, assessment, and future directions also are addressed' (Falender et al., 2004: 772).

Competency development in this context is seen as a lifelong learning enterprise (Falender and Shafranske, 2012b).

A 'supervision competencies framework' resulted from the Falender et al. (2004) working group, detailing the broad areas of knowledge, skill, attitudes and values required for competency, as detailed in Table 13.1.

Table 13.1 Falender et al.'s (2004) supervision competencies framework

Knowledge

1. Knowledge of area being supervised (psychotherapy, research, assessment, etc.)
2. Knowledge of models, theories, modalities and research on supervision
3. Knowledge of professional/supervisee development (how therapists develop, etc.)
4. Knowledge of ethics and legal issues specific to supervision
5. Knowledge of evaluation, process outcome
6. Awareness and knowledge of diversity in all its forms

Skills

1. Supervision modalities
2. Relationship skills: ability to build supervisory relationship/alliance
3. Sensitivity to multiple roles with supervisee and ability to perform and balance multiple roles
4. Ability to provide effective formative and summative feedback
5. Ability to promote growth and self-assessment in the trainee
6. Ability to conduct own self-assessment process
7. Ability to assess the learning needs and developmental level of the supervisee
8. Ability to encourage and use evaluative feedback from the trainee
9. Teaching and didactic skills
10. Ability to set appropriate boundaries and seek consultation when supervisory issues are outside domain of supervisory competence
11. Flexibility
12. Scientific thinking and the translation of scientific findings to practice throughout professional development

Values

1. Responsibility for client and supervisee rests with the supervisor
2. Respectful
3. Responsible for sensitivity to diversity in all its forms
4. Balance between support and challenging
5. Empowering
6. Commitment to lifelong learning and professional growth
7. Balance between clinical and training needs
8. Value ethical principles
9. Commitment to knowing and utilising available psychological science related to supervision
10. Commitment to knowing one's own limitations

(Continued)

Table 13.1 (Continued)

Social context overarching issues

1. Diversity
2. Ethical and legal issues
3. Developmental process
4. Knowledge of the immediate system and expectations within which the supervision is conducted
5. Awareness of the sociopolitical context within which the supervision is conducted
6. Creation of climate in which honest feedback is the norm (both supportive and challenging)

Training of supervision competencies

1. Coursework in supervision including knowledge and skill areas listed
2. Has received supervision of supervision, including some form of observation (videotape or audiotape) with critical feedback

Assessment of supervision competencies

1. Successful completion of course on supervision
2. Verification of previous supervision of supervision documenting readiness to supervise independently
3. Evidence of direct observation (e.g., audiotape or videotape)
4. Documentation of supervisory experience reflecting diversity
5. Documented supervisee feedback
6. Self-assessment and awareness of need for consultation when necessary
7. Assessment of supervision outcomes: both individual and group

Source: Falender et al. (2004: 778). Reproduced with the kind permission of John Wiley & Sons Inc. Copyright © 2004 Journal of Clinical Psychology, Wiley Periodicals Inc.

This framework is an excellent baseline resource for the training of supervisors, and advocates formal training as necessary for the development of competence in supervision. However, as this framework has been developed in a US context, where supervision is largely focused on trainee development, it may not address competencies required for working with more experienced practitioners in other cultural contexts. It provides an excellent framework for the supervisee to evaluate their supervisory experience. Nevertheless, further research and reflective practice are clearly indicated to address a number of practical questions. For example, in defining competencies from a technical rational perspective, might this be incongruent with and antithetical to the spirit of the supervisory process? What supervision training models would be most congruent to this endeavour? How might different practice contexts be best accommodated within a competency model?

Supervision Training Models

The rationale that has arisen in the professional and academic field for the formal training of supervisors has emerged from a number of considerations, for example:

- Supervisors need training to facilitate the development of supervisee competence (Milne and James, 2002; Gonsalvez and Milne, 2010).
- Supervision is a core competency in psychology (Falender et al., 2004; Inman and Soheilian, 2010).
- Supervision may be as challenging a competence to develop as therapy (Watkins, 1995).
- Perceptions of best practice (Green and Dye, 2002).
- Recommendations of training curricula (Borders et al., 1991; Getz, 1999; Milne and Westerman, 2001).
- Initiatives regarding evidence-based practice (e.g., Improving Access to Psychology Therapies; Milne and Reiser, 2012).

Many models exist for the training of supervisors. Bradley and Whiting (2001: 449) recommend that the following areas need to be included in supervision training curricula:

1. To provide a theory or knowledge base relevant to supervisory functioning.
2. To develop and refine supervisory skills.
3. To integrate the theory and skills into a working supervisory style.
4. To develop and enhance the professional identity of the supervisor.

The paradigm shift that is required to transition from practitioner to supervisor is not to be underestimated and is well captured in Watkins' (1990, 1993) Supervisor Complexity Model (SCM), which provides a four-stage model for supervisor development. This model outlines the various processes through which a supervisor transitions from 'role shock', through 'role recovery and transition' to 'role consolidation' and, finally, to 'role mastery' (Watkins, 1990: 556–8), which, in turn, are mediated by supervisor factors such as their 'developmental stage … personality factors, supervisor training/supervision, supervisor experience, and environmental supports' (Watkins, 1993: 60):

> *Stage 1: Role shock (and the imposter phenomenon)* (Watkins, 1990: 556): In this initial stage, the supervisor in training can feel like an 'imposter' as they struggle to come to grips with competence development, owning their professional authority and are focused more on content than process in the supervisory relationship.
> *Stage 2: Role recovery and transition* (Watkins, 1990: 556–7): As the supervisor gains experience, confidence is beginning to develop and the supervisor is engaging more deeply with the supervisee. There is an awareness of relational dynamics, but the supervisor does not yet feel confident enough to address these with the supervisee.
> *Stage 3: Role consolidation* (Watkins, 1990: 557–8): At this stage, greater self-awareness is demonstrated by the supervisor and a paradigm shift from therapist to supervisor has occurred. The supervisor identity is being integrated and there is more openness to experiencing. The supervisor can identify the clients' needs more clearly.
> *Stage 4: Role mastery* (Watkins, 1990: 558): This final stage is characterised by a balanced assessment of skills and the supervisor has become more flexible in their approach to supervision and in meeting their supervisees' learning needs. The supervisor has developed their own supervision style and is consistent in their theoretical approach.

Borders (2009: 127), who has been involved in the development of supervisor training curricula since 1989 (see Borders and Bernard, 1991; ACES, 1993), outlines the

'Principles of Best Practice for Supervision Training Programs'. In summary, Borders (2009: 128–50) recommends that supervision training courses should:

- 'Address all the core content areas identified in professional standards and the literature' (p. 128).
- 'Include both didactic instruction and supervised practice, concurrently and/or sequentially. Experiential activities should involve direct observation of supervision practice with feedback' (p. 130).
- 'Reflect a developmental approach in content and sequencing' (p. 136).
- 'Include instruction on a wide range of supervision methods, techniques, and approaches, with an emphasis on the intentional and flexible use of these approaches' (p. 140).
- 'Include instruction in basic principles of adult learning theory' (p. 142).

The outcomes of supervision training programmes are a further area of enquiry. In the UK context, with Improving Access to Psychology Therapies (IAPT) and National Institute for Clinical Excellence (NICE) guidelines, Bagnall and colleagues (2011) report on the National Health Service (NHS) Education for Scotland initiative of establishing supervision training for supervisors working within NHS Scotland to improve service provision. They outline the first stage as a course to develop generic supervision competencies for psychological therapy (which was piloted in 2009) and the second stage as providing for specialist competencies (e.g., cognitive behavioural therapy supervision). In their evaluation of the pilot training course (three-day course with 21 participants) in generic supervision skills, Bagnall et al. (2011) reported in general that there was a perceived increase in competence by the participants, most notably within the area of establishing and maintaining a supervisory alliance.

14

Developing the Art and Science of Supervision

This chapter considers some of the current issues regarding the art and science of supervision and proposes some areas for further research and development. It also provides reflection on the practitioner as researcher and what that means in the context of supervision.

Supervision Research and Development

The psychotherapy field has considered the nature of psychotherapy for many decades and, while not without some controversy, presents as both a science and an art (Schore, 2011). In the context of supervision, theory is slowly emerging, while the art of supervision is well developed. While many articles refer to the centrality of supervision in counselling and therapy training in particular, there is also the acknowledgement of the dearth of research in this area. Supervision research has developed well over the past few decades, although much of this emanates from the US trainee context which may not easily translate or be immediately relevant to the European context (Carroll, 1996). In particular, little is known about the post-qualification supervisee and how supervision may best serve their learning needs and, as mentioned, little is known about how or if supervision affects client welfare.

Notwithstanding the concerted call for empirical research in clinical supervision, the problems associated with existing supervision research have been well documented (Ellis and Ladany, 1997; Wheeler and Richards, 2007; Milne, 2009; Ladany and Malouf, 2010). Essentially, the supervisory relationship is a human relationship. As such, like any human relationship, the supervisory relationship comprises many complexities and variables which render it difficult to research, particularly as the supervisory situation encompasses the relationship, process and outcomes of therapy (Wheeler and Richards, 2007). Although researchers have sought to understand these complexities, it remains a difficult area of enquiry.

Other researchers have also highlighted additional deficits in supervision research relating to, for example, the use of invalidated measures, poor conceptualisation (Milne et al., 2008), a lack of a theoretical basis, and a lack of replication (Ellis et al., 1996) to mention just a few. The current state of supervision evidence seems a grim landscape. As mentioned earlier, and as suggested by Wheeler (2003), 'there is as yet scant evidence to support the effectiveness of supervision'; more recently, Wheeler noted that few studies have been practice based (Wheeler et al., 2011). To balance this picture, it is important to view this in context. Compared to psychotherapy research, supervision is still an emerging domain of enquiry and supervision research is in its infancy. Rather than that being a poor excuse for the lack of rigorous research, I suggest that it is an incentive for developing a research agenda in the field.

Timulak (2008: 164) suggests that supervision research has broadly charted process and outcome research in psychotherapy, with the majority of studies referring mainly to factors that facilitate or impede experiences of effective supervision. One of the contributing factors to this may be that supervision in Ireland and the UK has developed from work or practice-based knowledge rather than research (Holloway and Carroll, 1996). As practitioners, we have a rich tradition of practice-based knowledge, wisdom and insight in our community of practice. However, from my perspective, for supervision further to develop a balance between the art and science of supervision, a dialogical relationship between these knowledge bases is necessary (Hewson, 2001). This has been elegantly framed by Holloway (1995: 14) when she asserted that:

> The great potential before us as supervisors is to explicitly live out the connections between science knowledge and practice knowledge. The result will be a scientific practice that encompasses not just knowledge gained from traditional research, but also knowledge transferred from critical inquiry methods into our practice. Most of all, it is the articulation of our findings – what knowledge we use, how we are uncovering that knowledge, and how it is relevant to the immediacy of the client or supervisee dilemma – that is the heart of a systematic and deliberate supervisory process.

There is much to be discovered and many opportunities for a collaborative relationship to be developed among researchers and practitioners. Supervision in itself is a place where theory is applied to practice and critically reflected upon in terms of therapy and also in terms of supervision. As such, it is incumbent upon supervisors to be familiar with how research and practice can inform each other, and that this becomes a feature of work with supervisees and models a research attitude for their work with their clients. However, as Cooper (2010: 1) remarks, there appears to be reluctance among practitioners to embrace research. There are many hypotheses in the literature as to why this may be the case and a myriad of references to 'bridges' and 'gaps' between research and practice.

An engaging reflection on this dichotomy is provided by Wolfe (2012: 101), in an article entitled 'Healing the research–practice split: let's start with me'. The author enacts a two-chair dialogue between his 'therapist head' and his 'researcher head' in seeking to address the internal conflict he experiences in inhabiting both worlds and to find a creative solution. In acknowledging the inherent complexities in bridging the gap, not least of all the different epistemological stances of the therapist and the researcher, he recommends the following as a potential starting point (Wolfe, 2012: 106):

> By broadening the definition of valid research methodologies, finding ways of translating research findings into clinically useful therapeutic strategies, processes, and actions, and providing opportunities for clinical practitioners to study cases and videos of empirically supported therapies and therapeutic processes of change, we can make a good start on bridge building.

The stance of the practitioner-researcher, by its nature, seeks to address the research–practice gap – they live in the gap. It may be pertinent here to declare my own biases as they relate to research and practice. As an academic practitioner, it is important to me that research informs my practice. I understand practitioner research as a discovery-oriented method for knowledge to improve and advance practice. Research is a form of reflective practice. It can challenge our assumptions (Cooper, 2008) and 'habits of mind' (Mezirow, 2000: 7).

Considering Some of the Bridges and the Gaps

With increasing attention being paid to accountability, the promotion of evidence-based treatment and interventions, while somewhat divisive, are becoming the focus of many professional bodies and an area for reflection for therapists and supervisors alike (APA, 2006). Evidence-based practice is concerned with the systematic evaluation, under controlled conditions, of specific interventions and considers the efficacy of these (for example, randomised controlled trials (RCTs)). Practice-based evidence considers what happens in routine clinical practice and concerns itself with the effectiveness of treatment (Barkham and Mellor-Clark, 2000). This has interesting implications for working with supervisees, as they work with their clients, and how therapy process and outcome research may be reflected upon in supervision. With reference to supervision, Milne and colleagues (2011) provide a compelling argument for evidence-based clinical supervision, while also acknowledging the relevance of practice-based supervision research, a point supported by Wheeler et al. (2011), who also provide a compelling rationale for practice-based research.

To this end, Wheeler et al. (2011) discuss an initiative, in 2008, which the authors were instrumental in establishing in the UK and which was led by Professor Sue Wheeler. Funded by the BACP, a Supervision Practitioner Research Network (SuPReNet) was set up to promote supervision research. One of the key outcomes was the assessment and development of a 'supervision toolkit' (a set of supervision measures) for use by supervision practitioners and researchers. Such initiatives help standardise the use of measures in supervision research and allow for cross-study analysis, as well as making reliable research instruments more accessible to practitioners. One of these measures has already been mentioned previously, the Helpful Aspects of Supervision for Supervisors and Supervisees, adapted from Llewelyn's (1988) Helpful Aspects of

Therapy (HAT) form and reprinted, with the kind permission of the author of the original form, in Appendix 10.

As practitioners, we continually listen reflectively, engage in collaborative enquiry, collect data, form hypotheses about our supervisees or clients, analyse themes and patterns, revise our hypotheses when new information or evidence presents and are ever mindful of ethical nuances and issues. We engage in reflective practice and call on skills of reflexivity and critical reflection to do so. Hence, many of the skills of the researcher are already well developed and readily transferable to the research context (O'Brien and Houston, 2007; Creaner, 2011a).

In addition to the supervision research gaps mentioned throughout this book, most notably establishing the effectiveness of supervision in terms of therapy outcomes and therapist competence (Falender et al., 2013), there are many areas for further enquiry. We need to know how learning occurs in supervision and how it is transferred into therapy and how learning may best be facilitated and evaluated. This also needs to be established for supervision training. Further research on the interplay between relationship, process and outcome would serve to inform training and practice. Multicultural competence needs to be established. The experiences of senior practitioners are under-represented in the field and strategies for facilitating their learning need to be researched. The impact of organisations on supervision is indicated. As supervision research is an emerging focus, the possibilities for development are vast. There is, as Holloway (1995) encouraged, great potential before us.

Appendices

The appendices aim to provide useful resources for supervisees and supervisors:

1   Sample supervision learning agreement
2   Session pro forma documents
3   Codes of ethics and best practice guidelines for supervision
4   Supervision conferences
5   Sample of supervision training courses
6   Key journals for supervision-related articles
7   Sample of international supervision organisations
8   Supervision resources on the Internet
9   Holloway's (1995) process matrix
10 Helpful Aspects of Supervision forms
11 Sample of professional associations: accreditation/registration organisations

Appendix 1

Sample Supervision Learning Agreement

PRACTICALITIES OF SUPERVISION	
Introductions and professional background information (qualifications and experience of supervisor/supervisee)	
Context of supervision (training, pre-accreditation, consultancy)	
Frequency of supervision sessions	
Length of session	
Location	
Arrangements for cancellations/absences	
Fee	
Emergencies arrangements if supervisor is unavailable	
Length of supervision contract	
Termination of supervision	
Professional/training organization/agency requirements	
Third party contracts	
Professional indemnity insurance	
Supervisee informed consent (risks and benefits)	
Other considerations	
SUPERVISION RELATIONSHIP	
What are the supervisees'/supervisors' expectations of supervision?	

Role of the supervisee	
Role of the supervisor	
Responsibilities of the supervisee	
Responsibilities of the supervisor	
Theoretical orientation of supervisee/supervisor	
Code of professional ethics of supervisor/supervisee	
Supervisee and client confidentiality and privacy	
Multiple/dual relationship possibilities	
Complaints procedures and due process	
Record keeping procedures (supervision and therapy)	
How and when will our working relationship be reviewed?	
How/when will the learning agreement be reviewed?	
How will difficulties be addressed?	
THE SUPERVISION SESSION	
Supervisee current case load	
Client profile (e.g., adult, adolescent, child)	
Context of therapeutic work (general, trauma etc.)	
How will the supervision time be managed?	
How will client cases be presented? (Audio tapes/ transcripts/notes/etc.)	
Supervision methods (e.g., role-play, IPR, etc.)	
How will client-informed consent be provided?	
How will client progress and therapy outcomes be monitored?	
What are the risk management procedures?	
Professional and legal issues	
Diversity and inclusive practice considerations	
Framework for ethical decision making	
How will supervisee self-care be supported?	
Other	

SUPERVISEE LEARNING NEEDS	
What are the supervisees' learning preferences?	
Immediate developmental goals – Knowledge – Skill – Values/attitudes – Professional Identity	
Intermediate professional development plan for supervisee	
Longer term developmental goals – Knowledge – Skill – Values/attitudes – Professional identity	
How will feedback be given? Supervisee preferences?	
Other	
EVALUATION IN SUPERVISION	
What is the context of evaluation? (Training, accreditation, etc.)	
When will formal evaluation occur?	
What evaluation criteria will be used?	
Who will have access to evaluation reports?	
How will evaluation of supervisor/supervision experience take place?	
Other?	
Signed: Supervisee	
Signed: Supervisor	
Date:	**Review dates:**

Adapted from Carroll (1996: 98); Hawkins and Shohet (2012: 68); Sutter, McPherson and Geeseman (2002: 497–8); Thomas (2010: 152–61).

Appendix 2

Session Pro Forma Documents

Therapist: Client ID/Pseudonym:

Session date: _____   Time: _____

Session no.: _____

Client phenomena:

Presenting issue (state in client's words):

Client therapy goals:

Client history:

Clinical assessment:

Therapeutic relationship:

Therapeutic progress:

Client supports and resources:

Case conceptualisation:

Plans for next therapy session:

Therapist resources:

Learning needs for supervision:

Sample Supervision Session Reflection Pro Forma Document

Supervisor:	Supervisee code:	Number of sessions to date:
Learning goals for the supervision session:		
Brief reflection on context and content of session:		
Were your learning goals achieved?		
Plan for therapy on outcomes of supervision session? Actions required:		
Signed:		Date:

Appendix 3

Codes of Ethics and Best Practice Guidelines for Supervision

While the principles of all professional codes of ethics in counselling and psychotherapy apply to the practice of supervision, a number of professional organisations provide dedicated codes of ethics for supervision and/or guidelines for best practice in supervision. Below is a sample of those available.

American Association for Marriage and Family Therapy (AAMFT) (2012) Principle IV: Responsibility to Students and Supervisees. Available from: www.aamft.org/imis15/content/legal_ethics/code_of_ethics.aspx

American Association of Pastoral Counselors (AAPC) Code of Ethics (2012). Available from: www.aapc.org/policies/code-of-ethics.aspx

American Counseling Association (ACA) Code of Ethics (2005) Section F: Supervision, Training, and Teaching. Available from: www.counseling.org/Resources/aca-code-of-ethics.pdf

American Mental Health Counselors Association (AMHCA) Code of Ethics (2010) Section III: Commitment to Students, Supervisees and Employee Relationships. Available from: www.amhca.org/assets/content/AMHCA_Code_of_Ethics_2010_update_1-20-13_COVER.pdf

Association for Counselor Education and Supervision (ACES) (2011) Best Practices in Clinical Supervision. Available from: www.acesonline.net/wp-content/uploads/2011/10/ACES-Best-Practices-in-clinical-supervision-document-FINAL.pdf

Center for Credentialing and Education (CCE), the Approved Clinical Supervisor (ACS) Code of Ethics (2008). Available from: www.ncblpc.org/Laws_and_Codes/ACS_Code_of_Ethics.pdf

Irish Association for Counselling and Psychotherapy Code of Ethics and Practice for Supervisors (2005). Available from: www.irish-counselling.ie/Code-of-Ethics-for-Supervisors

Appendix 4

Supervision Conferences

International Interdisciplinary Conference on Clinical Supervision

This conference is held in the School of Social Work, Adelphi University, New York, in June each year. The conference is interdisciplinary in nature and focuses on clinical supervision theory, practice and research in the dissemination of new knowledge, research and best practices in the field of clinical supervision.

Further information is available from: http://socialwork.adelphi.edu/news-events/events/international-interdisciplinary-conference-on-clinical-supervision/

Association for Counselor Education and Supervision (ACES)

The ACES national conference is held bi-annually. In even years, each region hosts a conference. The 2013 Conference was held in Colorado in October. Further information is available from: www.acesonline.net/conference/

British Psychological Society

The first BPS Supervision Conference was held in April 2013. According to their website, 'this conference aims to promote excellence in supervision by providing a continuing professional development opportunity for those who supervise postgraduate psychology trainees'. BPS Divisions also hold regular conferences and a BPS Conference is held annually. Further information is available from: www.bps.org.uk/events/conferences

UKCP Annual Supervision Conference

For information, see: www.psychoanalytic-council.org/main/index.php?page=16203

Supervision Conference UK, formerly British Association for Supervision Practice and Research (BASPR)

This annual conference takes place in the UK and is focused on supervision practice and research. It is now organised by Oasis Talking Therapies CIC, Oasis-Talk, and further information may be found from: www.oasis-talk.org/professional-training/supervision-conference/

Other established conferences accept papers on supervision research and practice. For example:

British Association for Counselling and Psychotherapy (BACP) Conference

www.bacp.co.uk/research/events/

Society for Psychotherapy Research (SPR)

www.psychotherapyresearch.org/index.cfm

Society for the Exploration of Psychotherapy Integration (SEPI)

www.sepiweb.com/displaycommon.cfm?an=3

Psychological Society of Ireland (PSI)

www.psychologicalsociety.ie/conference/

Appendix 5

Sample of Supervision Training Courses

Academic Qualification and Professional Training: University-based Courses

Please note: This information is correct at time of writing. Please check directly with the relevant institutions for current information.

University: School of Psychology, Trinity College, Dublin, Ireland
Award: MSc/Postgraduate Diploma in Clinical Supervision
The MSc/Postgraduate Diploma in Clinical Supervision is a part-time course aimed at practitioners in the helping professions (e.g., qualified psychologists, psychotherapists, counsellors and mental health professionals) who wish to further their professional development, reflective practice and research capability and train as supervisors. On successful completion of Year 1, students may opt to exit with a Postgraduate Diploma award or, alternatively, proceed to Year 2 for the MSc route.
Website: http://psychology.tcd.ie/postgraduate/clinical-supervision/index.php

University: University of Derby
Award: Postgraduate Certificate in Clinical Supervision
This qualification is for people who aim to provide or are providing clinical supervision to counsellors or psychotherapists. This is a one-year, part-time, online course.
Website: www.derby.ac.uk/online/clinical-supervision-pg-cert

University: Teesside University
Award: Certificate in Postgraduate Professional Development: Clinical Supervision for Cognitive Behaviour Therapy Practice
The award prepares you for delivering CBT supervision to trainee or qualified therapists.
Website: www.tees.ac.uk/parttime_courses/Health_&_Social_Care/University_Certificate_in_Postgraduate_Professional_Development_Clinical_Supervision_for_Cognitive_Behaviour_Therapy_Practice.cfm

Training Institution: WPF Therapy (awards validated by Roehampton University)
Award: Postgraduate Diploma/MA in Supervision of Counselling and Psychotherapy
Website: www.wpf.org.uk/training/courses/courses/diploma-postgraduate-diploma-ma-in-supervision-of-counselling-and-psychotherapy.aspx

Training Institution: Institute for Arts in Therapy and Education
Award: Diploma in Child Counselling/Child Therapy/Child Psychotherapy Supervision (level of award according to previous qualifications)
Website: www.artspsychotherapy.org/child-therapy/diploma-in-child-counselling-child-therapy-child-psychotherapy-supervision

University: Keele University
Award: Postgraduate Certificate in Counselling Supervision
Website: www.keele.ac.uk/psychology/forapplicants/counsellingcourses/pgcertificate/

Training Institution: All Hallows College (award validated by Dublin City University)
Award: MA in Supervisory Practice
Website: www.allhallows.ie/programmes/postgrad/ma-in-supervisory-practice-new-for-2010.html

University: University of Chester, Department of Social Studies and Counselling
Award: Postgraduate Certificate in Counselling Supervision
Website: www.chester.ac.uk/postgraduate/counselling-supervision

University: University of Surrey
Award: MSc Supervision and Consultation: Psychotherapeutic and Organisational Approaches
Website:www.surrey.ac.uk/postgraduate/courses/socialsciences/psychologysupervision/index.htm

Professional Training and Continuing Professional Development (CPD) Courses

Many associations and organisations run CPD training workshops for their members. Other training institutes also offer professional training in supervision. Many are endorsed by professional organisations (e.g., meet with BACP criteria for inclusion on the register of supervisors). However, this needs to be verified directly with the training organisation. For example:

Training Institution: Metanoia Institute
Award: Certificate and Diploma in Supervision: An Integrative Relational Approach
Website: www.metanoia.ac.uk/integrative/Certdipsuperinteg
Award: Certificate/Diploma in Person Centred Supervision

Website: www.metanoia.ac.uk/person-centred/pcsuper
Award: Certificate/Diploma in clinical supervision for TA (transactional analysis) counsellors, CTAs (certified transactional analysts) and newly qualified PTSTAs (provisional teaching and supervising transactional analysts)
Website: www.metanoia.ac.uk/transactional-analysis/Post+Qualification+Training/ Certificate+and+Diploma+in+Clinical+Supervision/index
Award: Certificate/Diploma in Supervision: A Gestalt Relational Approach
Website: www.metanoia.ac.uk/gestalt/Gestalt+Supervision/index

Training Institution: Iron Mill Institute, Exeter, UK
Award: Diploma in Supervision
Website: www.ironmill.co.uk/cpd-course/diploma-in-supervision

British Association for Counselling and Psychotherapy

The BACP also runs a number of CPD online supervision modules for supervisor training (e.g., Supporting your supervisee through the accreditation process; Preparing for supervision and getting the most out of it).
Website: www.bacp.co.uk/accreditation/Accreditation%20(Counsellor%20&%20Psycho therapist)/supervisee.php
www.bacp.co.uk/cpd/cpd_search.php?view=all

The British Psychological Society

The BPS has many CPD and supervision training workshops.
Website: www.bps.org.uk

The Online Therapy Institute

The Online Therapy Institute currently provides online or in-person supervision training:
Website: http://onlinetherapyinstitute.com/approved-clinical-supervisor/

Appendix 6

Key Journals for Supervision-related Articles

British Journal of Guidance and Counselling: www.tandfonline.com/toc/cbjg20/current

The Clinical Supervisor: www.tandfonline.com/toc/wcsu20/current

The Counseling Psychologist: www.uk.sagepub.com/journals/Journal200805

Counselling Psychology Quarterly: www.tandfonline.com/toc/ccpq20/current

Counselling and Psychotherapy Research: www.tandfonline.com/toc/rcpr20/current

European Journal of Psychotherapy and Counselling: www.tandfonline.com/toc/rejp20/current

European Journal of Psychotherapy, Counselling and Health: www.ingentaconnect.com/content/routledg/rejp

International Journal for the Advancement of Counselling: www.springer.com/psychology/psychotherapy+%26+counseling/journal/10447

Journal of Counseling Psychology: www.apa.org/pubs/journals/cou/index.aspx

Person-centered and Experiential Psychotherapies: www.tandfonline.com/action/aboutThisJournal?show=editorialBoard&journalCode=RPCP

Professional Psychology: Research and Practice: www.apa.org/pubs/journals/pro/index.aspx

Psychotherapy Research: www.tandfonline.com/toc/tpsr20/current

Therapy Today (professional journal of the BACP): www.therapytoday.net/article/search/?searchstring=supervision

Appendix 7

Sample of International Supervision Organisations

The Association of National Organisations for Supervision in Europe (ANSE), according to their website, promotes and supports the development of quality assurance, training and research in supervision and coaching.

ANSE organises supervision summer universities and International Intervision groups across Europe. For further information, see: www.anse.eu

The Association for Counselor Education and Supervision (ACES) is a division of the American Counseling Association (ACA). It promotes 'quality education and supervision of counselors in all work settings'. For more information, see: www.acesonline.net/

The European Association for Supervision and Coaching (EASC) is an association for supervisors and coaches whose objectives are the promotion, application and quality assurance of supervision and coaching. For further information, see: www.easc-online. eu/index.php?id=11&L=1

Appendix 8

Supervision Resources on the Internet

The Supervision Centre
Prof. Michael Carroll's website provides excellent supervision resources:
www.supervisioncentre.com/

Centre for Supervision and Team Development
These websites provide information on professional supervision training courses, conferences and online resources for supervision:
www.cstd.co.uk/
www.cstdlondon.co.uk/
www.cstdbath.co.uk/

Carol Falender, PhD
This website provides many resources for supervisors and supervisees, including information on supervision books, supervision competencies, supervision measures, sample evaluation forms and supervision contract templates:
www.cfalender.com/supinfo.php

UCL Division of Psychology and Language Sciences
British Psychological Society's Centre for Outcomes Research and Effectiveness
Details of the Supervision Competences Framework are provided:
www.ucl.ac.uk/clinical-psychology/CORE/supervision_framework.htm

Online Therapy Institute
http://onlinetherapyinstitute.com/approved-clinical-supervisor/

TITL Magazine: *Therapeutic Innovations in Light of Technology*
http://issuu.com/onlinetherapyinstitute/docs/tiltissue13

Appendix 9

Holloway's (1995) Process Matrix

	Supervision tasks				
Functions	Counselling skills	Case conceptualisation	Professional role	Emotional awareness	Self-evaluation
Monitoring and evaluating					
Advising/ instructing					
Modelling					
Supporting/ sharing					
Consulting					

Source: Holloway (1995: 59). Reprinted with the permission of Sage Publications.

Appendix 10

Helpful Aspects of Supervision Forms*

HELPFUL ASPECTS OF SUPERVISION FORM (HAS) (10/93)

SUPERVISEES

Please complete this as soon after supervision as possible, and ideally no later than 24 hours after the supervision session.

Date:

Date of last supervision session:

Were you presenting a client today/yesterday? (please circle) Yes/No

Client contact hours to date: _____

1. Of the events that occurred in this session, which one do you feel was the most *helpful* to yourself and/or your work with your client(s)? (By 'event' we mean something that happened in the session. It might be something the supervisor or a fellow supervisee said or did.)

2. Please describe what made this event helpful/important and what you got out of it.

3. How helpful was this particular event? Rate it on the following scale. (Put an 'X' at the appropriate point; half-point ratings are OK; e.g., 7.5.)

_____

*Adapted from Liewelyn (1988) Helpful Aspects of Therapy (HAT) Form

```
HINDERING <-------------    Neutral    ------------->  HELPFUL
1       2       3       4       5       6       7       8       9
|---+---|---+---|---+---|---+---|---+---|---+---|---+---|---+---|
E       G       M       S               S       M       G       E
X       R       O       L               L       O       R       X
T       E       D       I               I       D       E       T
R       A       E       G               G       E       A       R
E       T       R       H               H       R       T       E
M       L       A       T               T       A       L       M
E       Y       T       L               L       T       Y       E
L               E       Y               Y       E               L
Y               L                               L               Y
                Y                               Y
```

4. About where in the session did this event occur?

5. About how long did the event last?

6. Did anything else particularly *helpful* happen during this session?
    YES/NO

    a. If yes, please rate how helpful this event was: _____ 6. Slightly helpful

                                                            _____ 7. Moderately helpful

                                                            _____ 8. Greatly helpful

                                                            _____ 9. Extremely helpful

    b. Please describe the event briefly:

7. Did anything happen during the session which might have been *hindering to you
    personally or to your work with your client(s)?*
    YES/NO

    a. If yes, please rate how hindering the event was: _____ 1. Extremely hindering

                                                            _____ 2. Greatly hindering

                                                            _____ 3. Moderately hindering

                                                            _____ 4. Slightly hindering

    b. Please describe this event briefly:

HELPFUL ASPECTS OF SUPERVISION FORM (HAS) (10/93)
(Copyright Sue Llewelyn)

SUPERVISORS

Please complete this as soon after supervision as possible, and ideally no later than 24 hours after the supervision session.

Date:

How many clients were presented today? _____

How many of your supervisees are seeing clients? _____

1. Of the events that occurred in this session, which one do you feel was the most *helpful* to a supervisee, and his or her work with clients? (By 'event' we mean something that happened in the session. It might be something you or a supervisee said or did or understood.)

2. Please describe what made this event helpful/important and what the supervisee got out of it.

3. How helpful was this particular event? Rate it on the following scale. (Put an 'X' at the appropriate point; half-point ratings are OK; e.g., 7.5.)

```
HINDERING <-------------     Neutral     -------------->  HELPFUL
   1       2       3       4       5       6       7       8       9
 |---+---|---+---|---+---|---+---|---+---|---+---|---+---|---+---|
   E       G       M       S               S       M       G       E
   X       R       O       L               L       O       R       X
   T       E       D       I               I       D       E       T
   R       A       E       G               G       E       A       R
   E       T       R       H               H       R       T       E
   M       L       A       T               T       A       L       M
   E       Y       T       L               L       T       Y       E
   L               E       Y               Y       E               L
   Y               L                               L               Y
                   Y                               Y
```

4. About where in the session did this event occur?

5. About how long did the event last?

6. Did anything else particularly *helpful* happen during this session?
   YES/NO

   a. If yes, please rate how helpful this event was: ____ 6. Slightly helpful

                                                                        ____ 7. Moderately helpful

                                                                        ____ 8. Greatly helpful

                                                                        ____ 9. Extremely helpful

   b. Please describe the event briefly:

7. Did anything happen during the session which might have been *hindering to a supervisee and his or her practice?*
   YES/NO

   a. If yes, please rate how hindering the event was: ____ 1. Extremely hindering

                                                                        ____ 2. Greatly hindering

                                                                        ____ 3. Moderately hindering

                                                                        ____ 4. Slightly hindering

   b. Please describe this event briefly:

Appendix 11

Sample of Professional Associations: Accreditation/Registration Organisations

Association of Child Psychotherapists (ACP): www.childpsychotherapy.org.uk

Association for Cognitive Analytic Therapy (ACAT): www.acat.me.uk

Association for Counselling and Therapy Online: www.acto-uk.org/index.htm

Association for Pastoral and Spiritual Care and Counselling (APSCC): www.apscc.org.uk

Association for Rational Emotive Behaviour Therapy (AREBT): www.arebt.net

British Association of Art Therapists (BAAT): www.baat.org

British Association for Behavioural and Cognitive Psychotherapies (BABCP): www.babcp.com

British Association for Counselling and Psychotherapy (BACP): www.bacp.org.uk

British Psychoanalytic Council (BPC): www.psychoanalytic-council.org

British Psychological Society (BPS): www.bps.org.uk

College of Sexual and Relationship Therapists (COSRT): www.cosrt.org.uk

Confederation of Scottish Counselling Agencies (COSCA): www.cosca.org.uk

Counsellors and Psychotherapists in Primary Care: www.cpc-online.co.uk

Federation of Drug and Alcohol Professionals (FDAP): www.fdap.org.uk

Health and Care Professions Council (HPCP): www.hpc-uk.org

Irish Association for Counselling and Psychotherapy (IACP): www.irish-counselling.ie

Psychological Society of Ireland (PSI): www.psihq.ie

United Kingdom Association of Humanistic Psychology Practitioners (UKAHPP): www.ahpp.org

United Kingdom Council for Psychotherapy (UKPC): www.psychotherapy.org.uk

Universities Psychotherapy and Counselling Association (UPCA): www.upca.org.uk

References

ACES (Association for Counselor Education and Supervision) (1993) Supervision Interest Network, ACES ethical guidelines for counseling supervisors. *ACES Spectrum*, 53 (4): 5–8.

Adair, S. (2001) Supervisor self-disclosure as a predicator of supervisee self-disclosure, satisfaction with supervision and perceptions of supervisor credibility. *Dissertation Abstracts International, Section B: The Sciences and Engineering*, 61: 4968.

Adams, D.M. (2009) Multicultural pedagogy in the supervision and education of psychotherapists. *Women and Therapy*, 33 (1–2): 42–54.

Adams, S.A. and Riggs, S. (2008) An exploratory study of vicarious trauma among therapist trainees. *Training and Education in Professional Psychology*, 2: 26–34.

Ainsworth, M.D.S. (1969) Object relations, dependency, and attachment: a theoretical review of the infant–mother relationship. *Child Development*, 40: 969–1025.

Ancis, J.R. and Marshall, D.S. (2010) Using a multicultural framework to assess supervisees' perceptions of culturally competent supervision. *Journal of Counseling and Development*, 88 (3): 277–84.

Anthony, K. and Goss, S. (2009) *Guidelines for Online Counselling and Psychotherapy*, 3rd edn. Rugby: BACP.

Anthony, K., Nagel, D.M. and Goss, S. (2010) *The Use of Technology in Mental Health*. Illinois: C.C. Thomas.

APA (American Psychological Association) (2006) Evidence-based practice in psychology: presidential task force on evidence-based practice. *American Psychologist*, 61 (4): 271–85.

Arcinue, F. (2009) The development and validation of the Group Supervision Scale. Unpublished doctoral dissertation, University of Southern California (2002) In J. Bernard and R. Goodyear, *Fundamentals of Clinical Supervision*, 4th edn. New Jersey: Pearson Merrill. p. 327.

Argyris, C. and Schön, D. (1974) *Theory in Practice: Increasing Professional Effectiveness*. California: Jossey-Bass.

Aten, J. and Couden-Hernandes, B. (2004) Addressing religion in clinical supervision: a model. *Psychotherapy: Theory, Research, Practice, Training*, 41 (2): 152–60.

BACP (British Association for Counselling and Psychotherapy) (2008) *What is Supervision?* S2:1 Information Sheet. London: BACP.

BACP (British Association for Counselling and Psychotherapy) (2012) Guidelines for expressing a grievance and making a complaint (www.bacp.co.uk/admin/structure/files/pdf/10530_guidance_grievance.pdf; retrieved 12 October 2012).

BACP (British Association for Counselling and Psychotherapy) (2013a) Applying for accreditation as a counsellor/psychotherapist: a guide for members (www.bacp.co.uk/admin/structure/files/pdf/11451_guide.pdf; retrieved 30 May 2013).

BACP (British Association for Counselling and Psychotherapy) (2013b) *Ethical Framework for Good Practice in Counselling and Psychotherapy.* Rugby: BACP.

BACP (British Association for Counselling and Psychotherapy) (2013c) Supervisor accreditation (www.bacp.co.uk/accreditation/Accreditation%20(Supervisor)/index.php; retrieved 17 September 2013).

Bagnall, G., Sloan, G., Platz, S. and Murphy, S. (2011) Generic supervision competencies for psychological therapies. *Mental Health Practice*, 14 (6): 18–23.

Bahrick, A., Russell, R. and Salmi, S. (1991) The effects of role induction on trainees' perceptions of supervision. *Journal of Counseling and Development*, 69: 434–8.

Bambling, M., King, R., Raue, P., Schweitzer, R. and Lambert, W. (2006) Clinical supervision: its influence on client-rated working alliance and client symptom reduction in the brief treatment of major depression. *Psychotherapy Research*, 16 (3): 317–31.

Barkham, M. and Mellor-Clark, J. (2000) Rigour and relevance: the role of practice-based evidence in the psychological therapies. In N. Rowland and S. Goss (eds), *Evidence-based Counselling and Psychological Therapies: Research and Applications.* London. Routledge. pp. 127–44.

Barnett, J.E., Erickson Cornish, J.A., Goodyear, R.K. and Lichtenberg, J.W. (2007) Commentaries on the ethical and effective practice of clinical supervision. *Professional Psychology: Research and Practice*, 38 (3): 268–75.

Baruch, V. (2009) Supervision groups in private practice: an integrative approach. *Psychotherapy in Australia*, 15 (3): 72–6.

Beinart, H. (2012) Models of supervision and supervisory relationship. In I. Fleming and L. Steen (eds), *Supervision and Clinical Psychology.* East Sussex, UK: Brunner-Routledge. pp. 47–63.

Belar, C.D., Brown, R.A., Hersch, L.E., Hornyak, L.M., Rozensky, R.H., Sheridan, E.P., Brown, R.T. and Reed, G.W. (2001) Self-assessment in clinical health psychology: a model for ethical expansion of practice. *Professional Psychology: Research and Practice*, 32: 135–41.

Berger, S.S. and Buchholz, E.S. (1993) On becoming a supervisee: preparation for learning in a supervisory relationship. *Psychotherapy: Theory, Research, Practice, Training*, 30: 86–92.

Bernard, J.M. (1979) Supervisor training: a discrimination model. *Counselor Education and Supervision*, 19 (1): 60–8.

Bernard, J.M. (1997) The discrimination model. In C.E Watkins (ed.), *Handbook of Psychotherapy Supervision.* New York: Wiley. pp. 310–27.

Bernard, J.M. (2006) Tracing the development of clinical supervision. *Clinical Supervisor*, 24 (1): 3–21.

Bernard, J. and Goodyear, R. (2009) *Fundamentals of Clinical Supervision*, 4th edn. New Jersey: Pearson-Merrill.

Berne, E. (1964) *Games People Play: The Basic Handbook of Transactional Analysis*. New York: Ballantine Books.

Bion, W.R. (1962) *Learning from Experience*. New York: Basic Books.

Bion, W.R. (1979/1987) Making the best of a bad job. In W.R. Bion, *Clinical Seminars and Four Papers*. Abingdon: Fleetwood Press. pp. 247–57.

Bogo, M. and Vayda, E. (1998) *The Practice of Field Instruction in Social Work: Theory and Process*, 2nd edn. New York: Columbia University Press.

Bond, T. (2013) Foreword. In M. Carroll and E. Shaw, *Ethical Maturity in the Helping Professions: Making Difficult Work and Life Decisions*. London: Jessica Kingsley. pp. 9–11.

Bond, T. and Mitchels, B. (2008) *Confidentiality and Record Keeping in Counselling and Psychotherapy*. London: Sage.

Borders, L.D. (1990a) Developmental changes during supervisees' first practicum. *Clinical Supervisor*, 8 (2): 157–67.

Borders, L.D. (1990b) Supervision not equal to evaluation. *School Counselor*, 37 (3): 253.

Borders, L.D. (1991) A systematic approach to peer group supervision. *Journal of Counseling and Development*, 69: 248–52.

Borders, L.D. (2006) Snapshot of clinical supervision in counseling and counselor education. *Clinical Supervisor*, 24 (1): 69–113.

Borders, L.D. (2009) Principles of best practice for clinical supervisor training programs. In J.R. Culbreth, and L.L. Brown (eds), *State of the Art in Clinical Supervision*. London. Routledge. pp. 127–50.

Borders, L.D. and Bernard, J.M. (1991) Curriculum guide for training counseling supervisors. *Counselor Education and Supervision*, 31 (1): 58.

Borders, L.D., Bernard, J.M., Dye, H.A., Fong, M.L., Henderson, P. and Nance, D.W. (1991) Curriculum guide for training counseling supervisors: rationale, development, and implementation. *Counselor Education and Supervision*, 31: 58–82.

Bordin, E.S. (1979) The generalizability of the psychoanalytic concept of the working alliance. *Psychotherapy: Theory, Research, and Practice*, 16: 252–60.

Bordin, E.S. (1983) A working alliance based model of supervision. *Counseling Psychologist*, 11: 35–41.

Bowlby, J. (1969) *Attachment and Loss*, vol. 1: *Attachment*. New York: Basic Books.

Bowlby, J. (1988) *A Secure Base*. New York: Basic Books.

Bowles, N. and Young, C. (1999) An evaluative study of clinical supervision based on Proctor's three function interactive model. *Journal of Advanced Nursing*, 30 (4): 958–64.

BPS (British Psychological Society) (2007) Division of Counselling Psychology, *Guidelines for Supervision*. London: BPS.

BPS (British Psychological Society) (2009) *Code of Ethics and Conduct: Guidance Published by the Ethics Committee of the British Psychological Society*. London: BPS (www.bps.org.uk/system/files/documents/code_of_ethics_and_conduct.pdf; retrieved 18 March 2013).

BPS (British Psychological Society) Ethics Committee (2012) *Supplementary Guidance on the Use of Social Media*. London: BPS (www.bps.org.uk/system/files/images/2012_ethics_committee_social_media.pdf; retrieved 3 July 2013).

Bradley, L.J. and Whiting, P.P. (2001) Supervision training: a model. In L.J. Bradley and N. Ladany (eds), *Counselor Supervision: Principles, Process, and Practice*, 3rd edn. Philadelphia, PA: Brunner-Routledge. pp. 361–88.

Bradley, L.J., Ladany, N., Hendricks, B., Whiting, P.P. and Rhode, K.M. (2010) Overview of counseling supervision. In N. Ladany and L.J. Bradley (eds), *Counselor Supervision*, 4th edn. New York: Routledge. pp. 3–13.

Brewer, G., Williams, A. and Sher, W. (2007) Utilising learning contracts to stimulate student ownership of learning. *Proceedings of the 2007 AseE Conference*, Melbourne (http://ww2.cs.mu.oz.au/aaee2007/papers/paper_88.pdf; retrieved 17 July 2013).

Bucky, S.F., Marques, S., Daly, J., Alley, J. and Karp, A. (2010) Supervision characteristics related to the supervisory working alliance as rated by doctoral-level supervisees. *Clinical Supervisor*, 29 (2): 149–63.

Burkard, A.W., Knox, S., Hess, S.A. and Schultz, J. (2009) Lesbian, gay, and bisexual supervisees' experiences of LGB-affirmative and non-affirmative supervision. *Journal of Counseling Psychology*, 56: 176–88.

Burton, W.H. (1930) Supervision. *American Journal of Nursing*, 30 (8): 1045–52.

Candy, P.C., Crebert, R.G. and O'Leary, J.O. (1994) *Developing Lifelong Learners through Undergraduate Education*. Canberra: National Board of Employment, Education and Training.

Carifio, M.S. and Hess, A.K. (1987) Who is the ideal supervisor? *Professional Psychology: Research and Practice*, 18 (3): 244–50.

Carr, W. (1995) *For Education: Towards Critical Educational Enquiry*. Buckingham: Open University.

Carrington, G. (2004) Supervision as a reciprocal learning process. *Educational Psychology in Practice*, 20 (1): 31–42.

Carroll, L., Gilroy, P.J. and Murra, J. (1999) The moral imperative: self-care for women psychotherapists. *Women and Therapy*, 22: 133–43.

Carroll, M. (1996) *Counselling Supervision: Theory, Skills and Practice*. London: Cassell.

Carroll, M. (2001) The spirituality of supervision. In M. Carroll and M. Tolstrup (eds), *Integrative Approaches to Supervision*. London: Jessica Kingsley. pp. 76–89.

Carroll, M. (2007) One more time: what is supervision? *Psychotherapy in Australia*, 13 (3): 34–40.

Carroll, M. (2009) Supervision: critical reflection for transformational learning, part 1. *Clinical Supervisor*, 28 (2): 210–20.

Carroll, M. (2010) Supervision: critical reflection for transformational learning, part 2. *Clinical Supervisor*, 29 (1): 1–19.

Carroll, M. and Gilbert, M. (2011) *On Being a Supervisee: Creating Learning Partnerships*, 2nd edn. London: Vukani.

Carter, J.W., Enyedy, K.C., Goodyear, R.K., Arcinue, F. and Puri, N.N. (2009) Concept mapping of the events supervisees find helpful in group supervision. *Training and Education in Professional Psychology*, 3 (1): 1–9.

Casement, P. (1985) *On Learning from the Patient*. London: Routledge.

Cashwell, C.S. (1994) *Interpersonal Process Recall*. Eric Digest, ERIC Clearinghouse on Counseling and Student Services, Greensboro, North Carolina. ED372342 (www.ericdigests.org/1995-1/recall.htm; retrieved 12 December 2010).

Cashwell, T. and Dooley, K. (2001) The impact of supervision on counselor self-efficacy. *Clinical Supervisor*, 20 (1): 39–47.

Cassidy, S. (2004) Learning styles: an overview of theories, models, and measures. *Educational Psychology: An International Journal of Experimental Educational Psychology*, 24 (4): 419–44.

Champe, J. and Kleist, D.M. (2003) Live supervision: a review of the research. *Family Journal*, 11 (3): 268–75.

Coker, J.K., Jones, W.P., Staples, P.A. and Harbach, R.L. (2002) Cybersupervision in the first practicum: implications for research and practice. *Guidance and Counselling*, 18: 33–8.

Coles, C. (2007) Personal growth and professional development. *Journal of Vocational Education and Training*, 59 (1): 89–105.

Cooney, L. (2010) Endings in clinical supervision as experienced by trainee counselling psychologists. MSc dissertation, Trinity College Dublin.

Cooper, M. (2008) *Essential Research Findings in Counselling and Psychotherapy: The Facts are Friendly*. London: Sage.

Cooper, M. (2010) The challenge of counselling and psychotherapy research. *Counselling and Psychotherapy Research*, 10 (3): 183–91.

Copeland, P., Dean, R.G. and Wladkowski, S.P. (2011) The power dynamics of supervision: ethical dilemmas. *Smith College Studies in Social Work*, 81 (1): 26–40.

Copeland, S. (1998) Counselling supervision in organisational contexts: new challenges and perspectives. *British Journal of Guidance and Counselling*, 26 (3): 377–86.

Copeland, S. (2002) Professional and ethical dilemmas experienced by counselling supervisors: the impact of organisational context. *Counselling and Psychotherapy Research*, 2 (4): 231–7.

Copeland, S. (2005) *Counselling Supervision in Organisations*. London: Routledge.

Couchon, W. and Bernard, J. (1984) Effects of timing of supervision on supervisor and counselor performance. *Clinical Supervisor*, 2 (3): 3–20.

Creaner, M. (2008) What is good supervision? Unpublished DPsych dissertation, Middlesex University/Metanoia Institute, London.

Creaner, M. (2011a) Reflections on learning and transformation in supervision. In R. Shohet (ed.), *Supervision as Transformation: A Passion for Learning*. London: Jessica Kingsley. pp. 146–59.

Creaner, M. (2011b) Handling and processing a referral. In R. Bor and M. Watts (eds), *The Trainee Handbook*, 3rd edn. London: Sage. pp. 51–69.

Creaner, Glen, J. and Creaner, M. (2010) Using learning agreements to facilitate integrated learning. Paper presented at the NAIRTL/LIN Annual Conference: Flexible Learning, Royal College of Surgeons, Dublin, October 6–7 (www.nairtl.ie/workgroupDocs/Brochure%202010SMALL.pdf; retrieved 5 April 2011).

Crick, P. (1991) Good supervision: on the experience of being supervised. *Psychoanalytic Psychotherapy*, 5 (3): 235–45.

Crook Lyon, R.E. and Potkar, K.A. (2010) The supervisory relationship. In N. Ladany and L.J. Bradley (eds), *Counselor Supervision*, 4th edn. New York: Routledge. pp. 15–52.

Cutcliffe, J., Butterworth, T. and Proctor, B. (eds) (2001) *Fundamental Themes in Clinical Supervision*. London: Routledge.

Cuthbert, P.F. (2005) The student learning process: learning styles or learning approaches? *Teaching in Higher Education*, 10 (2): 235–49.

Davies, J. (2009) Psychotherapy and the third wave of professionalisation. *European Journal of Psychotherapy and Counselling*, 11 (2): 191–202.

Davy, J. (2002) Discursive reflections on the research agenda for clinical supervision. *Psychology and Psychotherapy: Theory, Research and Practice*, 75: 221–38.

Davys, A. and Beddoe, L. (2010) *Best Practice in Supervision: A Guide for the Helping Professions*. London: Jessica Kingsley.

Department of Health/Mental Health Division/APT (2008) *Commissioning IAPT for the Whole Community: Improving Access to Psychological Therapies*. London: Department of Health.

De Stefano, J., D'Iuso, N., Blake, E., Fitzpatrick, M., Drapeau, M. and Chamodraka, M. (2007) Trainees' experiences of impasses in counselling and the impact of group supervision on their resolution: a pilot study. *Counselling and Psychotherapy Research*, 7 (1): 42–7.

Dickson, J.M., Moberly, N.J., Marshall, Y. and Reilly, J. (2011) Attachment style and its relationship to working alliance in the supervision of British clinical psychology trainees. *Clinical Psychology and Psychotherapy*, 18 (4): 322–30.

Doehrman, M. (1976) Parallel processes in supervision and psychotherapy. *Bulletin of the Menninger Clinic*, 40: 9–104.

Donaldson, S.I., Gooler, L.E. and Scriven, M. (2002) Strategies for managing evaluation anxiety: toward a psychology of program evaluation. *American Journal of Evaluation*, 23 (3): 261–73.

Dressel, J.L., Consoli, A.J., Kim, B.K. and Atkinson, D.R. (2007) Successful and unsuccessful multicultural supervisory behaviors: a Delphi poll. *Journal of Multicultural Counseling and Development*, 35 (1): 51–64.

Duff, A. and Duffy, T. (2002) Psychometric properties of Honey and Mumford's Learning Style Questionnaire (LSQ). *Personality and Individual Differences*, 22: 147–63.

Efstation, J.F., Patton, M.J. and Kardash, C.M. (1990) Measuring the working alliance in counselor supervision. *Journal of Counseling Psychology*, 37: 322–9.

Ekstein, R. and Wallerstein, R.S. (1958) *The Teaching and Learning of Psychotherapy*. New York: Basic Books.

Ekstein, R. and Wallerstein, R.S. (1972) *The Teaching and Learning of Psychotherapy*, 2nd edn. New York: International Universities Press.

Ellis, M.V. (2001) Harmful supervision, a cause for alarm: comment on Gray et al. (2001) and Nelson and Friedlander (2001). *Journal of Counseling Psychology*, 48 (4): 401–6.

Ellis, M.V. (2010) Bridging the science and practice of clinical supervision: some discoveries, some misconceptions. *Clinical Supervisor*, 29 (1): 95–116.

Ellis, M.V. and Ladany, N. (1997) Inferences concerning supervisees and clients in clinical supervision. In C.E. Watkins (ed.), *Handbook of Psychotherapy Supervision*. New York: Wiley. pp. 447–507.

Ellis, M.V., Ladany, N., Krengal, M. and Schult, D. (1996) Clinical supervision research from 1981 to 1993: a methodological critique. *Journal of Counseling Psychology*, 43: 35–50.

Emerson, S. (1996) Creating a safe place for growth in supervision. *Contemporary Family Therapy: An International. Journal*, 18: 393–403.

Enyedy, K.C., Arcinue, F., Puri, N.N., Carter, J.W., Goodyear, R.K. and Getzelman, M.A. (2003) Hindering phenomena in group supervision: implications for practice. *Professional Psychology: Research and Practice*, 34: 312–17.

Eraut, M. (1994) *Developing Professional Knowledge and Competence*. London: Falmer Press.

Falender, C.A. and Shafranske, E.P. (2004) *Clinical Supervision: A Competency-based Approach*. Washington, DC: American Psychological Association.

Falender, C.A. and Shafranske, E. (2007) Competence in competency-based supervision practice: construct and application. *Professional Psychology: Research and Practice*, 38 (3): 232–40.

Falender, C.A. and Shafranske, E.P. (2012a) *Getting the Most Out of Clinical Training and Supervision*. Washington, DC: American Psychological Association.

Falender, C.A. and Shafranske, E.P. (2012b) The importance of competency-based clinical supervision and training in the twenty-first century: why bother? *Journal of Contemporary Psychotherapy*, 42 (3): 129–37.

Falender, C.A., Burnes, T.R. and Ellis, M.V. (2013) Multicultural clinical supervision and benchmarks: empirical support informing practice and supervisor training. *Counseling Psychologist*, 41 (1): 8–27.

Falender, C.A., Erickson Cornish, J.A., Goodyear, R., Hatcher, R., Kaslow, N.J., Leventhal, G., Shafranske, E., Sigmon, S.T., Stoltenberg, C. and Grus, C. (2004) Defining competencies in psychology supervision: a consensus statement. *Journal of Clinical Psychology*, 60 (7): 771–85.

Falvey, J.E. and Cohen, C.R. (2003) The buck stops here. *Clinical Supervisor*, 22 (2): 63–80.

Farber, B.A. (2003) Self-disclosure in psychotherapy practice and supervision: an introduction. *Journal of Clinical Psychology*, 59 (5): 525–8.

Faure, E., Herrera, F., Kaddoura, A.-R., Lopes, H., Petrovsky, A.V., Rahnema, M. and Ward, F.C. (1972) *Learning to Be: The World of Education Today and Tomorrow*. Paris, France: UNESCO (http://unesdoc.unesco.org/images/0000/000018/001801e.pdf; retrieved 20 March 2012).

Feltham, C. (2000) Counselling supervision: baselines, problems and possibilities. In B. Lawton and C. Feltham (eds), *Taking Supervision Forward*. London: Sage. pp. 5–24.

Fitch, J.C., Pistole, C.M. and Gunn, J.E. (2010) The bonds of development: an attachment-caregiving model of supervision. *Clinical Supervisor*, 29 (1): 20–34.

Fleming, L.M., Glass, J.A., Fujisaki, S. and Toner, S.L. (2010) Group process and learning: a grounded theory model of group supervision. *Training and Education in Professional Psychology*, 4 (3): 194–203.

Folkes-Skinner, J., Elliott, R. and Wheeler, S. (2010) 'A baptism of fire': a qualitative investigation of a trainee counsellor's experience at the start of training. *Counselling and Psychotherapy Research*, 10 (2): 83–92.

Fook, J. (2012) *Social Work: A Critical Approach to Practice*, 2nd edn. London: Sage.

Foster, J., Lichtenberg, J. and Peyton, V. (2007) The supervisory attachment relationship as a predictor of the professional development of the supervisee. *Psychotherapy Research*, 17 (3): 343–50.

Fowler, J. and Chevannes, M. (1998) Evaluating the efficacy of reflective practice within the context of clinical supervision. *Journal of Advanced Nursing*, 27 (2): 379–82.

Frawley-O'Dea, M. and Sarnat, J. (2001) *The Supervisory Relationship: A Contemporary Psychodynamic Approach*. New York: Guilford Press.

Freire, P. (1970) *Pedagogy of the Oppressed*. New York: Seabury.

Freitas, G. (2002) The impact of psychotherapy supervision on client outcome: a critical examination of two decades of research. *Psychotherapy: Theory, Research, Practice, Training*, 39: 354–67.

Friedlander, M.L. and Ward, L. (1984) Development and validation of the supervisory styles inventory. *Journal of Counselling Psychology*, 4: 541–57.

Gardner, H. (1993) *Multiple Intelligences: The Theory in Practice*. New York: Basic Books.

Gatmon, D., Jackson, D., Koshkarian, L., Martos-Perry, N., Molina, A., Patel, N. and Rodolfa, E. (2001) Exploring ethnic, gender, and sexual orientation variables in supervision: do they really matter? *Journal of Multicultural Counseling and Development*, 29 (2): 102–13.

Gazzola, N. and Theriault, A. (2007) Super- (and not-so-super-)vision of counsellors-in-training: supervisee perspectives on broadening and narrowing processes. *British Journal of Guidance and Counselling*, 35 (2): 189–204.

Getz, H.G. (1999) Assessment of clinical supervisor competencies. *Journal of Counseling and Development*, 77: 491–7.

Gibbs, P. (2009) Learning agreements and work-based higher education. *Research in Post Compulsory Education*, 14 (1): 31–41.

Gilbert, M. and Evans, K. (2000) *Psychotherapy Supervision: An Integrative Relational Approach to Psychotherapy Supervision*. Buckingham: Open University Press.

Gilliam, T.H. and Armstrong, S.A. (2012) Spirituality and counseling supervision: current practices of board approved supervisors. *Clinical Supervisor*, 31: 25–41.

Glass, L.L. (2003) The gray areas of boundary crossings and violations. *American Journal of Psychotherapy*, 57 (4): 429–44.

Glickauf-Hughes, C. and Campbell, L.F. (1991) Experiential supervision: applied techniques for a case presentation approach. *Psychotherapy: Theory, Research, Practice, Training*, 28 (4): 625–35.

Gonsalvez, C.J. and Milne, D.L. (2010) Clinical supervisor training in Australia: a review of current problems and possible solutions. *Australian Psychologist*, 45 (4): 233–42.

Goodson, I. (2003) *Professional Knowledge, Professional Lives*. Buckingham: Open University Press.

Goodyear, R.K., Murdock, N., Lichtenberg, J.W., McPherson, R., Koetting, K. and Petren, S. (2008) Stability and change in counseling psychologists' identities, roles, functioning, and career satisfaction across 15 years. *Counseling Psychologist*, 36: 220–49.

Gould, L.J. and Bradley, L.J. (2001) Evaluation in supervision. In L.J. Bradley and N. Ladany (eds), *Counselor Supervision: Principles, Process, and Practice*, 3rd edn. Philadelphia, PA: Brunner-Routledge. pp. 271–303.

Grant, J. and Schofield, M. (2007) Career-long supervision: patterns and perspectives. *Counselling and Psychotherapy Research*, 7 (1): 3–11.

Gray, L.A., Ladany, N., Walker, J.A. and Ancis, J.R. (2001) Psychotherapy trainees' experience of counterproductive events in supervision. *Journal of Counseling Psychology*, 48: 371–83.

Green, D. and Dye, L. (2002) How should we best train clinical psychology supervisors? A Delphi survey. *Psychology Learning and Teaching* 2 (2): 108–15.

Green, H. (2011) Skills training and self-esteem: educational and clinical perspectives on giving feedback to clinical trainees. *Behaviour Change*, 28 (2): 87–96.

Green, M.S. and Dekkers, T.D. (2010) Attending to power and diversity in supervision: an exploration of supervisee learning outcomes and satisfaction with supervision. *Journal of Feminist Family Therapy*, 22 (10): 293–312.

Gregurek, R. (2007) Internal and external boundaries of supervision. *Group Analysis*, 40 (2): 167–77.

Guest, P. and Beutler, L. (1988) Impact of psychotherapy supervision on therapist orientation and values. *Journal of Consulting and Clinical Psychology*, 56 (5): 653–8.

Hahn, W. (2001) The experience of shame in psychotherapy supervision. *Psychotherapy*, 38 (3): 227–82.

Harbin, J.J., Leach, M.M. and Eells, G.T. (2008) Homonegativism and sexual orientation matching in counseling supervision. *Counselling Psychology Quarterly*, 21 (1): 61–73.

Harrison, R.L. and Westwood, M.J. (2009) Preventing vicarious traumatization of mental health therapists: identifying protective practices. *Psychotherapy*, 46 (2): 203–19.

Hart, G.M. (1982) *The Process of Clinical Supervision*. Baltimore: University Park Press.

Hattie, J. and Timperley, H. (2007) The power of feedback. *Review of Educational Research*, 77 (1): 81–112.

Haugaard Jacobsen, C. (2007) A qualitative single case study of parallel processes. *Counselling and Psychotherapy Research*, 7 (1): 26–33.

Haugaard Jacobsen, C. and Tanggaard, L. (2009) Beginning therapists' experiences of what constitutes good and bad psychotherapy supervision with a special focus on individual differences. *Nordic Psychology*, 61 (4): 59–84.

Hawkins, P. and Shohet, R. (2012) *Supervision in the Helping Professions*, 4th edn. Maidenhead, Berkshire: Open University Press.

Hawthorne, L. (1975) Games supervisors play. *Social Work*, 20 (3): 179–83.

HCPC (Health and Care Professions Council) (2012a) *Fitness to Practise Annual Report 2012*. London: HCPC (www.hpc-uk.org/assets/documents/10003D31Fitnesstopractis eannualreport2012.pdf; retrieved 16 October 2012).

HCPC (Health and Care Professions Council) (2012b) *The Fitness to Practise Process: Information for Employers and Managers.* London: HCPC (www.hpc-uk.org/assets/documents/10001FC8TheFTPprocess_cfw.pdf; retrieved 14 August 2013).

Heckman-Stone, C. (2004) Trainee preferences for feedback and evaluation in clinical supervision. *Clinical Supervisor,* 22 (1): 21–33.

Hernández, P. and McDowell, T. (2010) Intersectionality, power and relational safety: key concepts in clinical supervision. *Training and Education in Professional Psychology,* 4 (1): 29–35.

Heron, J. (1996) *Co-operative Inquiry: Research into the Human Condition.* London: Sage.

Hess, A.K. (1987) Psychotherapy supervision: Stages, Buber and a theory of relationship. *Professional Psychology: Research and Practice,* 18: 251–9.

Hess, S.A., Knox, S., Schultz, J.M., Hill, C.E., Sloan, L., Brandt, S., Kelley, F. and Hoffman, M.A. (2008) Predoctoral interns' nondisclosure in supervision. *Psychotherapy Research,* 18 (4): 400–11.

Hewson, D. (1999) Empowerment in supervision. *Feminism and Psychology,* 9: 406–9.

Hewson, J. (2001) Integrative supervision: art and science. In M. Carroll and M. Tolstru (eds), *Integrative Approaches to Supervision.* London: Jessica Kingsley. pp. 65–75.

Hill, C.E., Charles, D. and Reed, K.G. (1981) A longitudinal analysis of counseling skills during doctoral training in counseling psychology. *Journal of Counseling Psychology,* 28: 428–36.

Hill, C.E., Sullivan, C., Knox, S. and Schlosser, L. (2007) Becoming psychotherapists: experiences of novice therapists in a beginning graduate class. *Psychotherapy: Theory, Research, Practice, Training,* 44: 434–49.

Hoffman, M.A., Hill, C.E., Holmes, S.E. and Freitas, G.F. (2005) Supervisor perspective on the process and outcome of giving easy, difficult, and no feedback to supervisees. *Journal of Counseling Psychology,* 52: 3–13.

Hogan, R.A. (1964) Issues and approaches in supervision. *Psychotherapy: Theory, Research, and Practice,* 1: 139–41.

Holloway, E.L. (1987) Developmental models of supervision: is it development? *Professional Psychology: Research and Practice,* 19: 138–40.

Holloway, E.L. (1992) Supervision: a way of teaching and learning. In S.D. Brown and R.W. Lent (eds), *Handbook of Counseling Psychology.* New York: John Wiley. pp. 177–214.

Holloway, E.L. (1995) *Clinical Supervision: A Systems Approach.* Thousand Oaks, CA: Sage.

Holloway, E.L. and Carroll, M. (1996) Reactions to the special section on supervision research: comment on Ellis et al. (1996), Ladany et al. (1996), Neufeldt et al. (1996) and Worthen and McNeill (1996). *Journal of Counselling Psychology,* 43 (1): 51–5.

Holloway, E.L. and Wolleat, P.L. (1994) Supervision: the pragmatics of empowerment. *Journal of Educational and Psychological Consultation,* 5: 23–43.

Honey, P. and Mumford, A. (1982) *The Manual of Learning Styles.* Maidenhead, Berks: Honey Press.

Honey, P. and Mumford, A. (2000) *The Learning Styles Questionnaire: 80 Item Version.* Maidenhead, Berks: Peter Honey.

Horrocks, S. and Smaby, M.H. (2006) The supervisory relationship: its impact on trainee personal and skills development. In G.R. Walz, J.C. Bleuer and R.K. Yep (eds), *Compelling Perspectives on Counselling: VISTAS 2006.* Alexandria, VA: American Counseling Association. pp. 173–6.

Howard, E.E., Inman, A.G. and Altman, A.N. (2006) Critical incidents among novice counsellor trainees. *Counselor Education and Supervision*, 46: 88–102.

Howard, F. (1997) Supervision. In H. Love and W. Whittaker (eds), *Practice Issues for Clinical and Applied Psychologists in New Zealand.* Wellington: New Zealand Psychological Society. pp. 340–58.

Howard, F. (2008) Managing stress or enhancing wellbeing? Positive psychology's contributions to clinical supervision. *Australian Psychologist*, 43 (2): 105–13.

HPC (Health Professions Council) (2008) *Continuing Fitness to Practise: Towards an Evidence-based Approach to Revalidation.* London: HPC (www.hpc-uk.org/assets/documents/10002AAEContinuingfitnesstopractise-Towardsanevidence-basedapproachtorevalidation.pdf; retrieved 6 January 2013).

Hutt, C.H., Scott, J. and King, M. (1983) A phenomenological study of supervisees' positive and negative experiences in supervision. *Psychotherapy: Theory, Research, and Practice*, 20: 118–23.

Inman, A.G and Soheilian, S.S. (2010) Training supervisors: a core competency. In N. Ladany and L.J. Bradley (eds), *Counselor Supervision*, 4th edn. New York: Routledge. pp. 413–35.

Inskipp, F. and Proctor, B. (1995) *The Art, Craft and Tasks of Counselling Supervision.* Twickenham: Cascade.

Inskipp, F. and Proctor, B. (2001) *Becoming a Supervisor.* Twickenham: Cascade.

Jacobs, L. (2006) The supervision needs and experiences of accredited counsellors and psychotherapists working in Ireland. MSc dissertation, Trinity College Dublin.

Jarmon, H. (1990) The supervisory experience: an object relations perspective. *Psychotherapy: Theory, Research, Practice, Training*, 27 (2): 195–201.

Jenkins, P. (2007) *Counselling, Psychotherapy and the Law*, 2nd edn. London: Sage.

Johnston, L.H. and Milne, D.L. (2012) How do supervisees learn during supervision? A grounded theory study of the perceived developmental process. *Cognitive Behaviour Therapist*, 5: 1–23.

Jones-Boggs Rye, K. (2008) Perceived benefits of the use of learning contracts to guide clinical education in respiratory care students. *Respiratory Care*, 53 (11): 1475–81.

Kadushin, A. (1968) Games people play in supervision. *Social Work*, 13: 23–32.

Kadushin, A. (1992) *Supervision in Social Work*, 3rd edn. New York: Columbia University Press.

Kagan, N. (1980) Influencing human interaction: eighteen years with IPR. In A. K. Hess (ed.), *Psychotherapy Supervision: Theory, Research, and Practice.* New York: Wiley. pp. 262–83.

Kagan, N. (1984) Interpersonal process recall: basic methods and recent research. In D. Larson (ed.), *Teaching Psychological Skills: Models for Giving Psychology Away.* Monterey, CA: Brooks/Cole. pp. 229–44.

Kavanagh, D.J., Spence, S.H., Wilson, J. and Crow, N. (2002) Achieving effective supervision. *Drug and Alcohol Review*, 21 (3): 247–52.

Knowles, M.S. (1968) Andragogy, not pedagogy. *Adult Leadership*, 16 (10): 350–2, 386.

Knowles, M.S. (1980) The *Modern Practice of Adult Education: From Pedagogy to Andragogy*. Chicago: Follett.

Knox, S., Burkard, A.W., Edwards, L.M., Smith, J.J. and Schlosser, L.Z. (2008) Supervisors' reports of the effects of supervisor self-disclosure on supervisees. *Psychotherapy Research*, 18: (5): 543–59.

Knox, S., Edwards, L.M., Hess, S.A. and Hill, C.E. (2011) Supervisor self-disclosure: supervisees' experiences and perspectives. *Psychotherapy*, 48 (4): 336–41.

Koenig, T.L. and Spano, R.N. (2004) Sex, supervision, and boundary violations. *Clinical Supervisor*, 22 (1): 3–19.

Kolb, D.A. (1984) *Experiential Learning: Experience as the Source of Learning and Development*. Englewood Cliffs, NJ: Prentice Hall.

Kolb, D.A. (1976/1985) *Learning Style Inventory: Technical Manual*. Boston, MA: McBer.

Ladany, N. and Lehrman-Waterman, D.E. (1999) The content and frequency of supervisor self-disclosures and their relationship to supervisor style and the supervisory working alliance. *Counselor Education and Supervision*, 38(3): 143–60.

Ladany, N. and Malouf, M.A. (2010) Understanding and conducting supervision research. In N. Ladany and L.J. Bradley (eds), *Counselor Supervision*, 4th edn. New York: Routledge. pp. 353–88.

Ladany, N. and Walker, J.A. (2003) Supervisor self-disclosure: balancing the uncontrollable narcissist with the indomitable altruist. *Journal of Clinical Psychology*, 59 (5): 611–21.

Ladany, N., Ellis, M. and Friedlander, M. (1999) The supervisory working alliance, trainee self-efficacy and satisfaction. *Journal of Counseling and Development*, 77: 447–55.

Ladany, N., Mori, Y. and Mehr, K.E. (2013) Effective and ineffective supervision. *Counseling Psychologist*, 41 (1): 28–47.

Ladany, N., Walker, J.A. and Melincoff, D.S. (2001) Supervisor style, the supervisory working alliance, and supervisor self-disclosures. *Counselor Education and Supervision*, 40: 263–75.

Lamagna, J. (2011) Of the self, by the self and for the self: internal attachment, attunement and psychological change. *Journal of Psychotherapy Integration*, 21 (3): 280–307.

Langs, R. (1994) *Doing Supervision and Being Supervised*. London: Karnac Books.

Leddick, G.R. (1994) *Models of Clinical Supervision*. ERIC Digest, ERIC Clearinghouse on Counselling and Student Services, Greensboro, NC (www.ericdigests.org/1995-1/models.htm; retrieved 26 March 2013).

Leddick, G.R. and Bernard, J.M. (1980) The history of supervision: a critical review. *Counselor Education and Supervision*, 19: 186–96.

Lehrman-Waterman, D. and Ladany, N. (2001) Development and validation of the evaluation process within supervision inventory. *Journal of Counseling Psychology*, 48 (2): 168–77.

LeShan, L. (1996) *Beyond Technique: Psychotherapy for the 21st Century.* Northvale, NJ: Jason Aronson.

Lesser, R.L. (1983) Supervision: illusions, anxieties and questions. *Contemporary Psychoanalysis*, 18: 1–19.

Liddle, B. (1986) Resistance in supervision: a response to perceived threat. *Counselor Education and Supervision*, 26: 117–27.

Lidmila, A. (1997) Shame, knowledge and modes of enquiry in supervision. In G. Shipton (ed.), *Supervision of Psychotherapy and Counselling: Making a Place to Think.* Buckingham: Open University Press. pp. 35–46.

Linton, J.M. and Hedstrom, S.M. (2006) An exploratory qualitative investigation of group processes in group supervision: perceptions of masters-level practicum students. *Journal for Specialists in Group Work*, 31: 51–72.

Lizzio, A., Stokes, L. and Wilson, K. (2005) Approaches to learning in professional supervision: supervisee perceptions of processes and outcome. *Studies in Continuing Education*, 27 (3): 239–56.

Llewelyn, S.P. (1988) Psychological therapy as viewed by clients and therapists. *British Journal of Clinical Psychology*, 27: 223–37.

Lochner, B.T. and Melchert, T.P. (1997) The relationship of cognitive style and theoretical orientation to preferences for supervision in psychology interns. *Journal of Counseling Psychology*, 44: 256–60.

Loganbill, C., Hardy, E. and Delworth, U. (1982) Supervision: a conceptual model. *Counseling Psychologist*, 10: 3–42.

Lombardo, L.T., Greer, J., Estadt, B. and Cheston, S. (1998) Empowerment behaviors in clinical training. *Clinical Supervisor*, 16 (2): 33–47.

Luchner, A.F., Moser, C.J., Mirsalimi, H. and Jones, R.A. (2008) Maintaining boundaries in psychotherapy: covert narcissistic personality characteristics and psychotherapists. *Psychotherapy: Theory, Research, Practice, Training*, 45: 1–14.

McAdams III, C.R. and Wyatt, K. (2010) The regulation of technology-assisted distance counseling and supervision in the United States: an analysis of current extent, trends, and implications. *Counselor Education and Supervision*, 49 (3): 179–92.

McCarthy Veach, P. (2001) Conflict and counterproductivity in supervision: when relationships are less than ideal. Comment on Nelson and Friedlander (2001) and Gray et al. (2001). *Journal of Counseling Psychology*, 48 (4): 396–400.

McGee, T. (2005) Ethical and legal considerations in the training of mental health professionals. *Journal of Aggression, Maltreatment and Trauma*, 11 (3): 271–85.

Mackenzie, A. and Hamilton, R. (2007) More than expected? Psychological outcomes from first-stage training in counselling. *Counselling Psychology Quarterly*, 20 (3): 229–45.

McMahon, A. and Errity, D. (2013) From new vistas to life lines: psychologists' satisfaction with supervision and confidence in supervising. *Clinical Psychology and Psychotherapy* (doi: 10.1002/cpp.1835).

McNeill, B.W. and Worthen, V. (1989) The parallel process in psychotherapy supervision. *Professional Psychology: Research and Practice*, 20 (5): 329–33.

Magnuson, S., Wilcoxon, S. and Norem, A. (2000) A profile of lousy supervision: experienced counselors' perspectives. *Counselor Education and Supervision*, 30 (3): 189–202.

Mårtenson, D. and Schwab, P. (1993) Learning by mutual commitment: broadening the concept of learning contracts. *Medical Teacher*, 15 (1): 11.

Martin, C., Godfrey, M., Meekums, B. and Madill, A. (2011) Managing boundaries under pressure: a qualitative study of therapists' experiences of sexual attraction in therapy. *Counselling and Psychotherapy Research*, 11 (4): 248–56.

Mastoras, S. and Andrews, J. (2011) The supervisee experience of group supervision: implications for research and practice. *Training and Education in Professional Psychology*, 5: 102–11.

Mehr, K.E., Ladany, N. and Caskie, G.I.L. (2010) Trainee nondisclosure in supervision: what are they not telling you? *Counselling and Psychotherapy Research*, 10 (2): 103–13.

Merriam, S.B. (2008) Adult learning theory for the twenty-first century. *New Directions for Adult & Continuing Education*, 119: 93–8.

Mezirow, J. (ed.) (2000) *Learning as Transformation*. San Francisco, CA: Jossey-Bass/Wiley.

Miehls, D. (2010) Contemporary trends in supervision theory: a shift from parallel process to relational and trauma theory. *Clinical Social Work Journal*, 38 (4): 370–8.

Milne, D. (2009) *Evidence-based Clinical Supervision: Principles and Practice*. Oxford: Wiley Blackwell.

Milne, D. and James, I. (2002) The observed impact of training on competence in clinical supervision. *British Journal of Clinical Psychology*, 41: 55–72.

Milne, D. and Oliver, V. (2000) Flexible formats of clinical supervision: description, evaluation and implementation. *Journal of Mental Health*, 9 (3): 291–304.

Milne, D. and Reiser, R.P. (2012) A rationale for evidence-based clinical supervision. *Journal of Contemporary Psychotherapy*, 42 (3): 139–49.

Milne, D. and Westerman, C. (2001) Evidence-based clinical supervision: rationale and illustration. *Clinical Psychology and Psychotherapy*, 8: 444–5.

Milne, D., Aylott, H., Fitzpatrick, H. and Ellis, M.V. (2008) How does clinical supervision work? Using a 'best evidence synthesis' approach to construct a basic model of supervision. *Clinical Supervisor*, 27 (2): 170–90.

Milne, D., Pilkington, J., Gracie, J. and James, I. (2003) Transferring skills from supervision to therapy: a qualitative and quantitative n1 analysis. *Behavioural and Cognitive Psychotherapy*, 31: 193–202.

Milne, D., Sheikh, A.I., Pattison, S. and Wilkinson, A. (2011) Evidence-based training for clinical supervisors: a systematic review of 11 controlled studies. *Clinical Supervisor*, 30 (1): 53–71.

Mitchels, B. and Bond, T. (2010) *Essential Law for Counsellors and Psychotherapists*. London: Sage/BACP.

Moncayo, R. (2006) Lacanian perspectives on psychoanalytic supervision. *Psychoanalytic Psychology*, 23: 27–541.

Morrissey, J. and Tribe, R. (2001) Theory and practice: parallel process in supervision. *Counselling Psychology Quarterly*, 14 (2): 103–10.

Mothersole, G. (1999) Parallel process. *Clinical Supervisor*, 18 (2): 107–21.

Munson, C.E. (2002) *Handbook of Clinical Supervision*, 3rd edn. New York: Haworth Social Work Practice Press.

Murphy, D. (2011) Unprecedented times in the professionalisation and state regulation of counselling and psychotherapy: the role of the Higher Education Institute. *British Journal of Guidance and Counselling*, 39 (3): 227–37.

Nellis, A.C., Hawkins, K.L., Redivo, M. and Way, S. (2011) Productive conflict in supervision. Paper based on a program presented at the 2011 ACES Conference, Nashville Tennessee, 26–28 October. *Ideas and Research You Can Use: VISTAS 2012* (www.counselingoutfitters.com/vistas/vistas12/Article_81.pdf; retrieved 10 June 2013).

Nelson, J.A., Nichter, M. and Henriksen, R. (2010) On-line supervision and face-to-face supervision in the counseling internship: an exploratory study of similarities and differences. *Ideas and Research You Can Use: VISTAS 2010* (http://counselingoutfitters.com/vistas/vistas10/Article_46.pdf; retrieved 23 August 2013).

Nelson, M. and Friedlander, M. (2001) A close look at conflictual supervisory relationships: the trainee's perspective. *Journal of Counseling Psychology*, 48: 384–95.

Nelson, M., Evans, A.L., Triggiano, P.J. and Barnes, K.L. (2008) Working with conflict in clinical supervision: wise supervisors' perspectives. *Journal of Counseling Psychology*, 55 (2): 172–84.

Neswald-McCalip, R. (2001) Development of the secure counsellor: case examples supporting Pistole and Watkin's (1995) discussion of attachment theory in counselling supervision. *Counselor Education and Supervision*, 42: 18–27.

Nicol, D. (2010) From monologue to dialogue: improving written feedback processes in mass higher education. *Assessment and Evaluation in Higher Education*, 35 (5): 501–17.

Nicol, D.J. and Macfarlane-Dick, D. (2006) Formative assessment and self-regulated learning: a model and seven principles of good feedback practice. *Studies in Higher Education*, 31: 199–218.

Nikolou-Walker, E. and Garnett, J. (2004) Work-based learning: a new imperative? Developing reflective practice in professional life. *Reflective Practice*, 5 (3): 297–312.

Noelle, M. (2002) Self-report in supervision: positive and negative slants. *Clinical Supervisor*, 21 (1): 125–34.

Norcross, J.C. (ed.) (2011) *Psychotherapy Relationships that Work*, 2nd edn. New York: Oxford University Press.

Norcross, J.C. and Guy, Jr, J.D. (2007) *Leaving it at the Office: A Guide to Psychotherapist Self-care*. New York: Guilford Press.

Norcross, J.C. and Guy, Jr, J.D., with Karg, R.S. (2007) Sustaining healthy escapes. In J.C. Norcross and J.D. Guy, Jr, *Leaving it at the Office: A Guide to Psychotherapist Self-care*. New York: Guilford Press. pp. 131–52.

Norcross, J.C. and Guy, Jr, J.D., with Laidig, J. (2007) Recognizing the hazards. In J.C. Norcross and J.D. Guy, Jr, *Leaving it at the Office: A Guide to Psychotherapist Self-care*. New York: Guilford Press. pp. 35–63.

Norcross, J.C. and Guy, Jr, J.D., with Turkson, M.A. (2007) Restructuring cognitions. In J.C. Norcross and J.D. Guy, Jr, *Leaving it at the Office: A Guide to Psychotherapist Self-care*. New York: Guilford Press. pp. 114–30.

Norem, K., Magnuson, S., Wilcoxon, S.A. and Arbel, O. (2006) Supervisees' contributions to stellar supervision outcomes. *Journal of Professional Counseling: Practice,
Theory, and Research*, 34 (1 and 2): 33–48.

O'Brien, M. and Houston, G. (2007) *Integrative Therapy: A Practitioner's Guide*, 2nd edn.
London: Sage.

Ogren, M.L. and Jonsson, C.O. (2003) Psychotherapeutic skill following group supervision according to supervisees and supervisors. *Clinical Supervisor*, 22 (1): 35–58.

Olson, M., Russell, C. and White, M. (2001) Technological implications for clinical
supervision and practice. *Clinical Supervisor*, 20 (2): 201–15.

Orlans, V. and Edwards, D. (2001) A collaborative model for supervision. In M. Carroll
and M. Tholstrup (eds), *Integrative Approaches to Supervision*. London: Jessica
Kingsley. pp. 76–89.

Orlinsky, D.E. and Rønnestad, M.H. (2005) *How Psychotherapists Develop: A Study of
Therapeutic Work and Professional Growth*. Washington, DC: American Psychological
Association.

Osborn, C.J. and Davis, T.E. (1996) The supervision contract: making it perfectly clear.
Clinical Supervisor, 14 (2): 121–34.

Page, S. and Wosket, V. (2001) *Supervising the Counsellor: A Cyclical Model*, 2nd edn.
Sussex: Brunner-Routledge.

Patterson, C.H. (1983) A client-centered approach to supervision. *Counseling
Psychologist*, 11 (1): 21–5.

Patton, M. and Kivlighan, D. (1997) Relevance of the supervisory alliance to the counseling alliance and to treatment adherence in counselor training. *Journal of Counseling
Psychology*, 44 (1): 108–15.

Phillips, G. and Kanter, C. (1984) Mutuality in psychotherapy supervision. *Psychotherapy*,
21 (2): 178–83.

Pickworth, G.E. and Schoeman, W.J. (2000) The psychometric properties of the Learning
Style Inventory and the Learning Style Questionnaire: two normative measures of
learning styles. *South African Journal of Psychology*, 30 (2): 44–52.

Pistole, C.M. and Fitch, J.C. (2008) Attachment theory in supervision: a critical incident
experience. *Counselor Education and Supervision*, 47: 193–205.

Pistole, C.M. and Watkins, E.C. (1995) Attachment theory, counseling process, and
supervision. *Counseling Psychologist*, 23 (3): 457–78.

Polanyi, M. (1966) *The Tacit Dimension*. New York: Doubleday Anchor.

Power, A. (2012) When a supervisee retires. *Psychodynamic Practice: Individuals, Groups
and Organisations*, 18 (4): 441–55.

Power, S. (2007) Boundaries and responsibilities in clinical supervision. In J. Driscoll
(ed.), *Practicing Clinical Supervision*, 2nd edn. Edinburgh: Baillière Tindall. pp. 53–71.

Prest, L.A., Darden, E.C. and Keller, J.F. (1990) 'The fly on the wall' reflecting team
supervision. *Journal of Marital and Family Therapy*, 16: 265–73.

Proctor, B. (1987) Supervision: a co-operative exercise in accountability In M. Marken
and M. Payne (eds), *Enabling and Ensuring: Supervision in Practice*. Leicester: National
Youth Bureau, Council for Education and Training in Youth and Community Work.
pp. 21–34.

Proctor, B. (1994) Supervision: competence, confidence, accountability. *British Journal of Guidance and Counselling*, 22 (3): 309–18.

Proctor, B. (2008) *Group Supervision: A Guide to Creative Practice.* Los Angeles, CA: Sage.

Quarto, C.J. (2003) Supervisors' and supervisees' perceptions of control and conflict in counseling supervision. *Clinical Supervisor*, 21 (2): 21–37.

Quintana, S.M. (1993) Toward an expanded and updated conceptualization of termination: implications for short-term, individual psychotherapy. *Professional Psychology: Research and Practice*, 24 (4): 426–32.

Raichelson, S.H., Herron, W., Primavera, L.H. and Ramirez, S.M. (1997) Incidence and effects of parallel process in psychotherapy supervision. *Clinical Supervisor*, 15 (2): 37–48.

Ramos-Sánchez, L., Esnil, E., Goodwin, A., Riggs, S., Osachy Touster, L., Wright, L.K., Ratanasiripong, P. and Rodolfa, E. (2002) Negative supervisory events: effects on supervision satisfaction and supervisory alliance. *Professional Psychology: Research and Practice*, 33 (2): 197–202.

Rasmussen, B. (2012) The effects of trauma treatment on the therapist. In S. Ringel and J.R. Brandell (eds), *Trauma: Contemporary Directions in Theory, Practice and Research*. London: Sage.

Remley, T. and Herlihy, B. (2009) *Ethical, Legal and Professional Issues in Counseling*, 3rd edn. Boston: Merrill.

Renfro-Michel, E.L. and Sheperis, C.J. (2009) The relationship between counseling supervisee attachment orientation and perceived bond with supervisor. *Clinical Supervisor*, 28 (2): 141–54.

Richards, K.C., Campenni, C. and Muse-Burke, J.L. (2010) Self-care and well-being in mental health professionals: the mediating effects of self-awareness and mindfulness. *Journal of Mental Health Counseling*, 32 (3): 247–64.

Richardson, S. (1987) Implementing contract learning in a senior nurse practicum. *Journal of Advanced Nursing*, 12 (2): 201–6.

Riva, M.T. and Cornish, E. (1995) Group supervision practices at psychology predoctoral internship programs: a national survey. *Professional Psychology: Research and Practice*, 26: 523–5.

Riva, M.T. and Erickson Cornish, J.A. (2008) Group supervision practices at psychology predoctoral internship programs: 15 years later. *Training and Education in Professional Psychology*, 2 (1): 18–25.

Rogers, C.R. (1951) *Client-centered Therapy: Its Current Practice, Implications and Theory*. Boston: Houghton Mifflin.

Rogers, C. and Freiberg, H. (1993) *Freedom to Learn*, 3rd edn. New York: Merrill.

Rønnestad, M.H. and Skovholt, T.M. (2001) Learning arenas for professional development: retrospective accounts of senior psychotherapists. *Professional Psychology: Research and Practice*, 32 (2): 181–7.

Roth, A.D. and Pilling, S. (2009) A competence framework for the supervision of psychological therapies (www.ucl.ac.uk/clinical-psychology/CORE/supervision_framework.htm; retrieved 14 August 2013).

Rubin, S. (1989) At the border of supervision: critical moments in psychotherapists' development. *American Journal of Psychotherapy*, 43 (3): 387–97.

Russell-Chapin, L.A. and Chapin, T.J. (2012) *Clinical Supervision: Theory and Practice*. Belmont, CA: Brooks Cole-Cengage Learning.

Safran, J., Muran, C., Stevens, C. and Rothman, M. (2007) A relational approach to supervision: addressing ruptures in the alliance. In C.A. Falender and E.P. Shafranske (eds), *Clinical Supervision: A Competency-based Approach*. Washington, DC: APA. pp. 137–57.

Scaife, J. (2001) *Supervision in the Mental Health Professions: A Practitioner's Guide*. Hove: Brunner-Routledge.

Schlesinger, H.J. (2005) *Endings and Beginnings: On the Technique of Terminating Psychotherapy and Psychoanalysis*. Hillsdale, NJ: Analytic Press.

Schön, D. (1983) *The Reflective Practitioner: How Professionals Think in Action*. Aldershot: Ashgate.

Schore, A.N. (2011) *The Science of the Art of Psychotherapy*. New York: W.W. Norton.

Scott, K., Ingram, K., Vitanza, S. and Smith, N. (2000) Training in supervision: a survey of current practices. *Counseling Psychologist*, 28: 403–22.

Scriven, M. (1967) The methodology of evaluation. In R.W. Tyler, R.M. Gagné and M. Scriven (eds), *Perspectives of Curriculum Evaluation*. Chicago, IL: Rand McNally. pp. 39–83.

Scriven, M. (1991) Beyond formative and summative evaluation. In M.W. McLaughlin and D.C. Phillips (eds), *Evaluation and Education: At Quarter Century*. Chicago: National Society for the Study of Education. pp. 19–64.

Searles, H.F. (1955) The informational value of supervisor's emotional experiences. *Psychiatry*, 18: 135–46.

Shallcross, R.L., Johnson, W.B. and Lincoln, S.H. (2010) Supervision. In J.C. Thomas and M. Hersen (eds), *Handbook of Clinical Psychology Competencies*. New York: Springer. pp. 503–48.

Shanfield, S.B., Hetherly, V. and Matthews, K.L. (2001) Excellent supervision: the residents' perspective. *Journal of Psychotherapy Practice and Research*, 10 (1): 23–7.

Shanfield, S.B., Matthews, K.L. and Hetherly, V. (1993) What do excellent psychotherapy supervisors do? *American Journal of Psychiatry*, 150: 1081–4.

Skovholt, T.M. and Jennings, L. (2004) *Master Therapists: Exploring the Expertise in Therapy and Counseling*. Boston: Allyn and Bacon.

Skovholt, T.M. and Rønnestad, M. (1992) *The Evolving Professional Self: Stages and Themes in Therapist and Counselor Development*. New York: Wiley.

Sobell, L.C., Manor, H.L., Sobell, M.B. and Dum, M. (2008) Self-critiques of audiotaped therapy sessions: a motivational procedure for facilitating feedback during supervision. *Training and Education in Professional Psychology*, 2 (3): 151–5.

Spence, D.P. (1986) Narrative smoothing and clinical wisdom. In T.R. Sarbin (ed.), *Narrative Psychology: The Storied Nature of Human Conduct*. New York: Praeger. pp. 211–32.

Stake, R.E. (2004) *Standards-based and Responsive Evaluation*. London. Sage.

Starling, P.V. and Baker, S.B. (2000) Structured peer group practicum supervision: supervisees' perceptions of supervision theory. *Counselor Education and Supervision*, 39: 162–76.

Steinhelber, J., Patterson, V., Cliffe, K. and LeGoullon, M. (1984) An investigation of some relationships between psychotherapy supervision and patient change. *Journal of Clinical Psychology*, 40 (3): 1346–53.

Stoltenberg, C.D. (1981) Approaching supervision from a developmental perspective: the counselor complexity model. *Journal of Counseling Psychology*, 28: 59–65.

Stoltenberg, C.D. (2005) Enhancing professional competence through developmental approaches to supervision. *American Psychologist*, 60 (8): 857–64.

Stoltenberg, C.D. and Delworth, U. (1987) *Supervision, Counselors and Therapists*. San Francisco: Jossey-Bass.

Stoltenberg, C.D. and McNeill, B.W. (1997) Clinical supervision from a developmental perspective: research and practice. In C.E. Watkins (ed.), *Handbook of Psychotherapy Supervision*. New York: Wiley. pp. 184–202.

Stoltenberg, C.D., McNeill, B.W. and Delworth, U. (1998) *IDM Supervision: An Integrated Developmental Model for Supervising Counselors and Therapists*. San Francisco: Jossey-Bass.

Stretch, L.S., Nagel, D. and Anthony, K. (2012) Ethical framework for the use of technology in supervision. *Therapeutic Innovations in Light of Technology*, 3 (2): 37–45 (http://issuu.com/onlinetherapyinstitute/docs/tiltissue13/37?e=1923820/1290177; retrieved 12 August 2013).

Strozier, A., Kivlighan, D. and Thoreson, R. (1993) Supervisor intentions, supervisee reactions and helpfulness: a case study of the process of supervision. *Professional Psychology: Research and Practice*, 24 (1): 13–19.

Sutter, E., McPherson, R. and Geeseman, R. (2002) Contracting for supervision. *Professional Psychology: Research and Practice*, 33 (5): 495–9.

Sweeney, J. and Creaner, M. (forthcoming) What's not being said? Recollections of nondisclosure in clinical supervision while in training. Manuscript submitted for publication.

Symons, C., Khele, S., Rogers, J., Turner, J. and Wheeler, S. (2011) Allegations of serious professional misconduct: an analysis of the British Association for Counselling and Psychotherapy's Article 4.6 cases, 1998–2007. *Counselling and Psychotherapy Research*, 11 (4): 257–65.

Tannenbaum, R. and Berman, M. (1990) Ethical and legal issues in psychotherapy supervision. *Psychotherapy in Private Practice*, 8 (4): 65–77.

Thériault, A. and Gazzola, N. (2005) Feelings of inadequacy, insecurity, and incompetence among experienced therapists. *Counselling and Psychotherapy Research*, 5 (1): 11–18.

Thomas, J. (2007) Informed consent through contracting for supervision: minimizing risks, enhancing benefits. *Professional Psychology: Research and Practice*, 38 (3): 221–31.

Thomas, J. (2010) *The Ethics of Supervision and Consultation: Practical Guidance for Mental Health Professionals*. Washington, DC: American Psychological Association.

Timulak, L. (2008) *Research in Psychotherapy and Counselling*. London: Sage.

Totton, N. (2010) Boundaries and boundlessness. *Therapy Today*, 21 (8): 10–15.

Tracey, T.J.G., Bludworth, J. and Glidden-Tracey, C.E. (2012) Are there parallel processes in psychotherapy supervision? An empirical examination. *Psychotherapy*, 49 (3): 330–43.

Usher, C.H. and Borders, L.D. (1993) Practicing counselors' preferences for supervisory style and supervisory emphasis. *Counselor Education and Supervision*, 33 (2): 66–79.

Vaccaro, N. and Lambie, G.W. (2007) Computer-based counselor-in-training supervision: ethical and practical implications for counselor educators and supervisors. *Counselor Education and Supervision*, 47 (1): 46–57.

Vallance, K. (2004) Exploring counsellor perceptions of the impact of counselling supervision on clients. *British Journal of Guidance and Counselling*, 32 (4): 559–74.

Van Ooijen, E. (2000) *Clinical Supervision: A Practical Guide.* Edinburgh: Churchill Livingstone.

Walker, J.A., Ladany, N. and Pate-Carolan, L.M. (2007) Gender-related events in psychotherapy supervision: female trainee perspectives. *Counselling and Psychotherapy Research*, 7 (1): 12–18.

Walker-Strong, C. (2011) What trainees want from clinical supervision. MSc thesis, Trinity College Dublin, Ireland.

Watkins, Jr, C.E. (1990) Development of the psychotherapy supervisor. *Psychotherapy*, 27: 553–60.

Watkins, Jr., C.E. (1993) Development of the psychotherapy supervisor: concepts, assumptions, and hypotheses of the Supervisor Complexity Model. *American Journal of Psychotherapy*, 47: 58–74.

Watkins, Jr, C.E. (1995) Pathological attachment styles in psychotherapy supervision. *Psychotherapy*, 32 (2): 333–40.

Watkins, Jr, C.E. (ed.) (1997) *Handbook of Psychotherapy Supervision.* New York: Wiley.

Watkins, Jr, C.E. (1998) Psychotherapy supervision in the 21st century: some pressing needs and impressing possibilities. *Journal of Psychotherapy Practice and Research*, 7 (2): 93–101.

Watkins, Jr, C.E. (2012) Psychotherapy supervision in the new millennium: competency-based, evidence-based, particularized, and energized. *Journal of Contemporary Psychotherapy*, 42 (3): 193–203.

Watkins, Jr, C.E. and Scaturo, D. (2013) Toward an integrative, learning-based model of psychotherapy supervision: supervisory alliance, educational interventions, and supervisee learning/relearning. *Journal of Psychotherapy Integration*, 23(1): 75–95.

Weaks, D. (2002) Unlocking the secrets of 'good supervision': a phenomenological exploration of experienced counsellors' perceptions of good supervision. *Counselling and Psychotherapy Research*, 2 (1): 33–9.

West, W. (2003) The culture of psychotherapy supervision. *Counselling and Psychotherapy Research*, 3 (2): 123–7.

Wheeler, S. (2003) *Research on Supervision of Counsellors and Psychotherapists: A Systematic Scoping Search.* Rugby: BACP.

Wheeler, S. and Richards, K. (2007) The impact of clinical supervision on counsellors and therapists, their practice and their clients; a systematic review of the literature. *Counselling and Psychotherapy Research*, 7 (1): 54–65.

Wheeler, S., Aveline, M. and Barkham, M. (2011) Practice-based supervision research: a network of researchers using a common toolkit. *Counselling and Psychotherapy Research*, 11 (2): 88–96.

Whiston, S. and Emerson, S. (1989) Ethical implications for supervisors in counseling of trainees. *Counselor Education and Supervision*, 28: 318–25.

Wilcoxon, A., Norem, K. and Magnuson, S. (2005) Supervisee's contributions to lousy supervision outcomes. *Journal of Professional Counseling Practice, Theory and Research*, 33 (2): 31–49.

Wilkerson, K. (2006) Peer supervision for the professional development of school counselors: toward an understanding of terms and findings. *Counselor Education and Supervision*, 46 (1): 59–67.

Williams, E.N., Judge, A., Hill, C.E. and Hoffman, M.A. (1997) Experiences of novice therapists in pre-practicum: trainees', clients' and supervisors' perceptions of therapists' personal reactions and management strategies. *Journal of Counseling Psychology*, 44: 390–9.

Winnicott, D. (1960) The theory of the parent–child relationship. *International Journal of Psychoanalysis*, 41: 585–95.

Wolfe, B.E. (2012) Healing the research–practice split: let's start with me. *Psychotherapy*, 49 (2): 101–8.

Wong, L.J., Wong, P. P. and Ishiyama, F. (2013) What helps and what hinders in cross-cultural clinical supervision: a critical incident study. *Counseling Psychologist*, 41(1): 66–85.

Worthen, V. and Dougher, M. (2000) Evaluating effective supervision. Paper presented at the 108th Annual Conference of the American Psychological Association (www.eric.ed.gov; ERIC no. ED446322; retrieved 10 July 2004).

Worthen, V. and McNeill, B. (1996) A phenomenological investigation of good supervision events. *Journal of Counselling Psychology*, 43 (1): 25–34.

Worthington, E.R. (2006) Changes in supervision as counselors and supervisors gain experience: a review. *Training and Education in Professional Psychology*, S (2): 133–60.

Worthington, R.L., Tan, J.A. and Poulin, K. (2002) Ethically questionable behaviors among supervisees: an exploratory investigation. *Ethics and Behavior*, 12 (4): 323–51.

Wosket, V. (2012) Clinical supervision. In C. Feltham and I. Horton (eds), *Sage Handbook of Counselling and Psychotherapy*. London: Sage. pp. 164–72.

Wosket, V. and Page, S. (2001) The cyclical model for supervision: a container for creativity and chaos. In M. Carroll and M. Tolstrup (eds), *Integrative Approaches to Supervision*. London: Jessica Kingsley. pp. 13–31.

Wulf, J. and Nelson, M.L. (2001) Experienced psychologists' recollections of internship supervision and its contributions to their development. *Clinical Supervisor*, 19 (2): 123–45.

Yegdich, T. (1999) Lost in the crucible of supportive clinical supervision: supervision is not therapy. *Journal of Advanced Nursing*, 29 (5): 1265–75.

Ziv-Beiman, S. (2013) Therapist self-disclosure as an integrative intervention. *Journal of Psychotherapy Integration*, 23 (1): 59–74.

Index

Page references to Figures or Tables will be in *italics*

www.ingramcontent.com/pod-product-compliance
Lightning Source LLC
Chambersburg PA
CBHW080359030426
42334CB00024B/2929